New Perspectives on Young Children's Moral Education

ALSO AVAILABLE FROM BLOOMSBURY

Teaching Virtue, edited by Marius Felderhof
Does Religious Education Work?, by James C. Conroy, David Lundie,
Robert A. Davis, Vivienne Baumfield, L. Philip Barnes, Tony Gallagher,
Kevin Lowden, Nicole Bourque and Karen Wenell
Reimagining Liberal Education, by Hanan Alexander
Ethical English, by Mark A. Pike

New Perspectives on Young Children's Moral Education

Developing character through a virtue ethics approach

Tony Eaude

Bloomsbury Academic
An imprint of Bloomsbury Publishing Plc

B L O O M S B U R Y

LONDON • OXFORD • NEW YORK • NEW DELHI • SYDNEY

Bloomsbury Academic
An imprint of Bloomsbury Publishing Plc

50 Bedford Square	1385 Broadway
London	New York
WC1B 3DP	NY 10018
UK	USA

www.bloomsbury.com

**BLOOMSBURY and the Diana logo are trademarks of
Bloomsbury Publishing Plc**

First published 2016

British Library Cataloguing-in-Publication Data
A catalogue record for this book is available from the British Library.

ISBN: HB: 978-1-4725-9647-5
PB: 978-1-4725-9646-8
ePDF: 978-1-4725-9648-2
ePub: 978-1-4725-9649-9

Library of Congress Cataloging-in-Publication Data
A catalog record for this book is available from the Library of Congress.

Typeset by Newgen Knowledge Works (P) Ltd., Chennai, India
Printed and bound in Great Britain

Contents

Acknowledgements

Many people have shaped my ideas in diverse, often unconscious, ways, and supported me in thinking about young children's education and ethics and in writing this book.

I am grateful to many colleagues with whom I have taught and discussed how young children learn and how adults can guide them in living thoughtful, unselfish and fulfilled lives. I admire those brave teachers and headteachers who continue to believe that all young children need a broad and balanced range of experiences and to create environments of trust, care and challenge within which they can flourish.

Richard Pring and Mark Halstead supervised my doctoral thesis and introduced me, in different ways, to the academic literature on morality and ethics and helped to broaden my rather narrow and all-too-certain perspective.

Geerthi Ahilan, Liz Burton, Jane Godby and Clare Whyles read drafts of chapters and made valuable comments based on their experience as a teacher or headteacher.

Many people at Bloomsbury have been involved in bringing the book to publication and these ideas to a wider audience.

My greatest debt is to Jude Egan, who has enabled me to understand the centrality of emotion, relationships and care, through her actions and her words and her love over twenty-eight years. She has always believed in, and supported, me and my work, even when others were sceptical or preoccupied with other matters.

My thanks to them all, and many other relatives, friends and colleagues too numerous to name.

Tony Eaude
tony.eaude@education.ox.ac.uk

Introduction

New Perspectives on Young Children's Moral Education encourages you to think in fresh ways about young children's moral education for the complex and changing world in which they grow up and will live as adults. The book does not aim to provide answers to specific moral problems or say how to manage children's behaviour or deliver a specific programme – and its concern with policy is indirect. Rather, it draws on a wide range of research related to ethics and young children's learning to prompt thinking about how children can learn to act and interact appropriately in a world where new, often unforeseen, challenges lie ahead.

The book is written mainly for educators, that is any adult with a responsibility for young children, including parents and carers, teachers and others, such as leaders of voluntary groups, whether based on a religious affiliation or any other activity. Given the varying beliefs about what morality entails, this book explores principles and strategies which can be adapted to different contexts, religious and secular, schools and other settings.

One distinctive feature is the focus on young children, up to about 11 or 12 years old. While the needs and responses of 10-year-olds differ from those of 6-, or 3-year-olds, age should, as we shall see, be one only factor affecting how adults act. I use the term 'middle childhood' to refer to what psychoanalysts call the latency phase, when children's focus moves from themselves towards a greater sense of being part of a group (or groups). Children are usually in this phase between the ages of 7 and 11 (or a bit earlier). I refer to 'early childhood' or very young children for those under the age of about 7.

How anyone approaches moral education depends on their beliefs and assumptions and the context. Inevitably, you will not share my beliefs and assumptions and will work in a different context. My background, described in more detail in Chapter 3, is as a teacher, headteacher and academic in England interested in young children's learning, particularly personal development, and how schools can enhance this. So, I write from this perspective, but try, linking research and practice, to identify lessons valuable for all adults, whatever their role, context or culture. For those whose experience is mainly with young children, one aim is to show how a moral dimension runs through every aspect of life. For those whose interest relates more to religion or ethics, I attempt to show how exploring young children's learning can enrich one's understanding of, and ways of working, in those areas.

People who write about morality and moral education tend to believe that they know what is right and wrong and how to teach children this, and try and persuade others how to do so, with varying degrees of subtlety. My approach, in contrast, rather than starting from a definite view of morality or how children should think about moral problems, focuses on how young children act and interact and learn to do so appropriately – whatever that means and whatever the context. Without an understanding of how young children learn, it is hard to know how they will learn to live appropriately. So, my approach is 'bottom-up', rather than 'top-down'.

I draw on various traditions of ethics to consider what adults working with young children can learn from these. Rather than being prescriptive, I present dilemmas, tensions and possible solutions, suggesting rather than preaching, inviting readers to think how the ideas fit with their own experience and may be applied in their own setting. This does not mean that I lack strong views. In particular, I believe that how individuals act and interact, and how society is organized and operates, matter profoundly; and that these are essentially moral questions.

New Perspectives on Young Children's Moral Education may be seen as like a tapestry, or a collage, or a guidebook. In the tapestry, threads of different colours and textures are interwoven, with the overall result becoming clear only gradually. In the collage, apparently unrelated ideas are collected and connected, building up a picture created from many images. As a guidebook, this book does not give detailed instructions for the journey, but suggests and describes places worth visiting, some familiar, some less so.

I try to discuss complex and contested ideas such as ethics, knowledge, character, virtues and values in relatively simple and accessible language. At times, this involves oversimplifying, but such a danger is unavoidable. The book covers a broad landscape, aspects of which may be unfamiliar. The ideas are intended to be thought-provoking and radical:

- challenging many current assumptions about ethics and education; and
- encouraging readers, whatever their background and beliefs, to question their own assumptions.

So, it may help to read slowly and reflectively and to try to suspend initial judgement on questions such as:

- whether children are naturally good or bad;
- whether in the past everything was wonderful or awful;
- what moral education entails; and
- what adults should do to enable this.

This is in the hope that you will emerge with new insights, without necessarily agreeing with everything I write.

My approach is broadly in line with Nel Noddings' (2013, p. 3) view that 'we may present a coherent and enlightening picture without *proving* anything and, indeed, without claiming to present or to seek moral *knowledge* or moral *truth*. The hand that steadied us as we learned to ride our first bicycle did not provide propositional knowledge but it guided and supported us all the same and we finished up "knowing how."' Or in Symington's (1986, p. 11) words, describing psychoanalysis, 'I am talking of a single reality but coming at it from different perspectives. This is the Hebrew rather than the Greek way of treating a human phenomenon. The Hebrew way is to go round and round a subject, each time using different images to illuminate what is most profound. The Greek way of arguing by logical stages can never, in my opinion, do justice to any deep experience.' So, the argument unfolds in a roundabout rather than a linear way.

Three main themes run through the book:

1 The current social and cultural climate results in children receiving strong, often conflicting, messages and pressures about how they should act, encouraging a view of success, happiness and identity as primarily based on external factors such as money, celebrity and image; and underplaying, or denying, the extent to which most actions have a moral component. We live in a time of moral uncertainty and confusion, for children and adults.

2 Educational policy, in England and elsewhere, has lost touch with the fundamentally moral nature of education and how young children learn. Increasingly, society and schools and settings, even for very young children, privilege cognitive processes and outcomes over emotional ones – intellect over feeling and attainment over care. The aims of education, in a pluralist democracy, are necessarily multifaceted and contested. Its main focus especially with young children, cannot, without damage, be reduced to the acquisition of factual knowledge

and attainment in what can be tested. Education must address the needs of the whole child, both as s/he is now and will be in the future. So, moral education must be developed throughout the life of any institution, not restricted to only some subject areas.

3 The discourse on ethics has been too dominated by rationalism and individualism rather than relationships and context. This is reflected in the current emphasis on individual actions, rational choice and conscious decisions, rather than the social nature of ethics, the pressures resulting from external influences and early and preconscious patterns of response. I argue for an approach based on embedding intrinsic motivation, on developing character and the virtues associated with living 'a good life', and incorporation into a moral community, rather than relying on simple notions of right and wrong and adult prescription.

In a nutshell, *New Perspectives on Young Children's Moral Education* suggests that most actions and interactions have a moral dimension; and that, if the word is to be meaningful, ethics involves action rather than just intention, for reasons that are largely intrinsic. If enabling children to live a good life is to be one central aim of education, every aspect of their upbringing and schooling has a moral dimension. To see moral education primarily as 'teaching children right from wrong' takes insufficient account of how young children learn and the extent to which acting appropriately requires judgement of the context. Since the roots of ethics lie in children's early experience, attributes and dispositions associated with character and virtue and the judgement about how and when to manifest these should be cultivated right from the start.

The book is in three main parts which explore in turn the context, the 'roots of' and 'routes into' moral education. Part I (Chapters 1–4) raises key debates and dilemmas and describes the main traditions of ethics and the changing social, cultural and educational context. This helps to:

- show different ways in which morality, and moral education, has been understood and the implications of this; and
- identify the mixed messages and often-intense pressures on children at an increasingly young age about how to act and interact.

The reasons why the moral dimension of education is currently underplayed, despite its historical importance and its place in legislation, are discussed. Recognizing the role and importance of religious traditions, I suggest that religion is not a sufficient basis for moral education in the public sphere in an increasingly diverse and secularized society. I caution adults against a sense of moral superiority, arguing that we should recognize and respect the qualities which young children manifest and that care for others is an essential foundation of ethics.

Part II (Chapters 5–7) draws on research into young children's learning to highlight the implications for education and ethics. The close link between emotion and cognition is emphasized. Preconscious mechanisms underpin and affect conscious ones, with the latter, such as the ability to exercise choice, developing only gradually and strongly influenced by early experience, anxiety and a range of external factors. Young children find abstract thought and self-regulation hard. The role of relationships, example, habituation and self-regulation, feedback and language and a sense of agency and identity, and the complex links between them, in how children learn to regulate their actions, are explored. External factors, and how children's background, culture and existing knowledge are valued, exert a strong influence on their motivation. Praise, affirmation and attention influence young children positively more than put-downs, punishment and competition. In Chapter 7, these learning processes are linked more specifically to ethics, considering how terms such as character, values and virtues identify attributes associated with 'living a good life' and can form the basis of a vocabulary of ethics. The idea of moral identity is considered as a changing narrative of who one is, and may become.

Part III (Chapters 8–10) discusses how adults can best help young children learn to act and interact appropriately, avoiding the pitfalls identified in Chapter 1 and building on the insights from Part II. Chapter 8 outlines the importance, and the features, of learning environments and the 'moral order', suggesting that a moral dimension should run through every aspect of provision. Chapter 9 explores activities, experience and responses, including the use of language, which particularly help to cultivate empathy and thoughtfulness. Chapter 10 considers why discrete programmes are of limited use unless backed by caring and trusting relationships and personal and institutional authenticity, with adults showing flexibility and exercising judgement. An approach based on virtue ethics and an apprenticeship model is suggested to help identify, and embed, the attributes children require to negotiate the challenges ahead.

The final chapter gathers the threads, summarizing some key implications for ethics, children, adults and, briefly, policy, if we are to help young children find a path through the confusing and challenging world they face, now and for a future about which we can only speculate.

Part I

The Context of Young Children's Moral Education

1

The Landscape
of Moral Education

Introducing the language
of morality and ethics

Recently, I suggested during a course on learning environments that one aspect worth considering was the moral environment. Immediately, an experienced and thoughtful nursery school headteacher responded that she thought it inappropriate to tell young children what was right and wrong and that she did not see this as part of her role.

I wonder how you respond to this incident, both whether you agree with the headteacher, and the idea of moral education and morality behind her view. Presumably, this involved 'telling' and 'right and wrong', even though I suspect she had strong views on how children should act and interact – and how to influence this.

Some people relate morality mainly to personal and private behaviour, others as permeating all, or most, of our lives and the social structures within which we operate. Some associate morality with courses of action to be forbidden, others those to be encouraged. And morality may be seen as mainly to do with intentions, or more related to outcomes. There is no consensus about the scope of morality.

The word 'moral' puts off many adults who care for and educate young children, like the headteacher above, while others may see a moral dimension as a central aspect of their role. Even those who do so may be unsure about what this involves. You may see moral education as primarily about adults controlling children's behaviour, or children being enabled to learn for themselves how they should act and interact. You may think of a code of conduct, perhaps based on a religious faith; or children learning to make choices based on principles such as rights and responsibilities or maxims like 'do as you would be done by.' You may be worried about indoctrination, or about relativism. Your approach may involve rewards, prohibitions and punishments, to encourage appropriate behaviour; or a less specific view based on the sort of person a child is and will become, related to ideas such as values and character. My guess is that your view may include several of these. But you may adopt a particular moral stance or believe that education should be only about academic learning rather than shaping children's character.

This brief discussion indicates that the landscape of morality, and moral education, is deeply contested, with little consensus about:

- what morality and ethics involves and to what extent morality is linked to religion;
- what moral education entails; and
- who is responsible for moral education,

all questions we shall explore.

Language both reflects and shapes how we think about children and childhood, about individuals and societies, about culture and religion. The language we use reflects our view of human nature, morality and education, such as whether we see children as fundamentally good, and to be enabled; or bad, and to be controlled. The metaphors and words we use reflect our beliefs, often without this being obvious to ourselves or to other people. For example, the current focus on 'behaviour management' is based on a behaviourist approach relying on stimulus and response, to ensure compliance, and adult control. I prefer the term 'conduct' to suggest that children should be expected to be responsible for their actions. Calls for improved discipline usually imply externally imposed expectations, backed up by punishment and, perhaps, reward. However, 'self-discipline' suggests individuals being able to regulate their own actions and make informed choices.

How language is used is particularly problematic in discussing morality, ethics and moral education, with many words having more than one meaning or unfamiliar or unfortunate resonances. For instance, thoughtfulness can mean both being reflective and being considerate. What people of one culture or generation understand by a word may have different connotations for those of another. Words such as character and virtue, previously in common use, may now be considered as somewhat archaic, and possibly suspect, evident in the recent trend to prefer the term values. Chapter 7 considers the reasons for this and advantages and disadvantages of such terms.

Let me explain how I use the terms moral and ethical. Noddings (2013, p. 27) writes that 'to behave ethically is to behave under the guidance of an acceptable and justifiable account of what it means to be moral'. Winston (1998, p. 21) cites Bernard Williams' description of 'thick concepts, specific ethical notions which constitute *a system of ethics* as opposed to *a morality system*'. So, I tend to use ethics and ethical to describe specific actions in context and morality and moral more generally. For instance, I write of moral dilemmas or the moral dimension, and of people living ethically and ethics as involving actions related to everyday life. However, in practice, how these two terms are used often overlaps.

So, what are morality and ethics about? Put simply, about 'shoulds' and 'oughts'. However, again we must be careful with language. Think how 'right' may be used to denote technical competence or approval. One may talk about holding a pencil or paintbrush 'in the right way', without suggesting that this is an ethical issue. In saying that it is not right to take another child's possessions without permission, one enters the domain of ethics. Calling a toddler 'naughty' may have various meanings from mild disapproval to a definite proscription. The boundary between a young child learning to act in a particular way for reasons of safety, efficiency or morality is far from clear. The word 'should' may imply just a suggestion, as it usually does in this book, or a stern precept.

The scope of morality and ethics is not clear-cut. Ethics is to some extent about individual action, but also about how people relate to each other and the sort of communities and societies we create. Most individuals exert only a tiny influence on how society is organized, but they can, and do, affect the groups in which they live. For adults, these may be mainly their family, workplace and local community, for children their family, friendship group, class or school.

Dewey (2002, p. 357) wrote that 'morals are as broad as acts which concern our relationship with others'. If so, the domain of morality and ethics would seem to encompass a wide range of human actions and interactions.

Let me illustrate this with two examples. Whether one should cycle through a red light when this poses no danger to oneself or others would be seen by some people not as a moral question, or at least not in any serious sense. Others would see it as breaching a code of conduct, though presumably doing so would be justifiable in some circumstances, like an emergency or if the lights are obviously not working. Whether to grow one's own vegetables might seem just a matter of inclination or preference, not of morality. But, when one considers the chemicals required, or whether the tomatoes or beans in a shop are genetically modified or have been flown in from distant countries, the distinction between moral and non-moral becomes more blurred.

To some extent, what is deemed appropriate depends on culture and context, rather than law or proscription. For instance, when in Finland, I was surprised that cars rarely exceeded the speed limit on open, rural roads; and my hosts were just as puzzled at my response on the grounds that 'people don't speed because they see and understand the point of the law'. The prime motivation was moral rather than legal, intrinsic rather than externally policed. As we shall see, for children to recognize *why* they should act in a particular way is both necessary and a powerful motivator to do so.

Most actions, and especially interactions, have both technical and ethical norms – how well they are performed and whether one should do them. Sergiovanni (2001, p. 14) captures this in distinguishing between 'doing things right and doing right things', that is:

- acting in ways that are right or appropriate; and
- doing well whatever one does.

If one is not doing the right thing, it would seem at best morally neutral, and probably worse, to do it well. So, for instance, to abuse someone on the basis of their skin colour, religion or gender would seem even more disgraceful if done very hurtfully; and filling in a false tax return in a convincing way more reprehensible than doing so ineptly. I suggest that 'doing right things' matters more than 'doing things right', that ethics should trump effectiveness, especially in activities involving other people.

Some moral questions seem clearly related to issues of right and wrong. For instance, it is hard to find any possible justification for attacking a stranger and stealing her purse; or for one child to bite or taunt another. However, the vast majority of ethical decisions are about what is better or worse rather than right or wrong; and what to do when two demands clash. Honesty is a virtue, but its application usually relates not so much to whether or not to be honest, but rather how honest to be towards a friend enquiring whether a dress which you dislike suits her, or a young child asking what you think of his smudged painting.

This example reflects an underlying philosophical debate about whether right action should be based on universal principles or depend on the context – in academic terms between universalism and particularism. Universalists argue that principles, such as justice, can be worked out by reason and then applied to any given situation, regardless of context. Particularists, in contrast, see the right course of action depending on the context and judging between competing claims as to how one should act. So, particularists believe that it may be right in some circumstances to steal – for instance if one is starving – and that one must often compromise between conflicting principles, say between justice and love, or honesty and mercy, whereas universalists tend to assert that it is wrong to steal and that the correct course of action can be decided by reasoning. Chapter 7 discusses the limitations of universalism, arguing that moral educators should seek to develop children's judgement based on the attributes associated with character and virtue.

What does moral education entail?

As Noddings (2013, p. 1) indicates, 'ethics . . . has concentrated for the most part on moral reasoning'. In contrast, this book sees ethics as about how people act and interact, rather than what they say, or think, or intend – although these often affect how they act. Pring writes (2014, p. 151) that 'beliefs are embodied in habits, dispositions and spontaneous actions as much as they are in declarations of belief', though I suggest that beliefs are embodied even more in unconscious than conscious processes. Moral education is not just about helping children to decide in principle whether to steal food when one is starving or to administer drugs to help someone in pain die quickly. While it may be interesting (at least to philosophers) to discuss such dilemmas, these very rarely, if ever, occur for individuals, particularly young children. Neither is moral education just a matter of encouraging good behaviour, or compliance, because of habit, fear or reward; but about the intrinsic motivation which influences conduct, more profoundly, in unfamiliar situations and in the long term.

Actions based solely on habit would not seem within the scope of ethics, but one may be hard-pressed at times to decide to what extent a young child's action is intentional. This raises the question of when children become moral agents. Most writing on morality assumes that there is a premoral period, assuming that morality and ethics involve intention, the exercise of conscious choice. A similar view is enshrined in law by decisions on the age of criminal responsibility, though the actual age varies between countries. Setting an age of moral responsibility is even more problematic. It cannot be that a child is not a moral agent one day, but is the next. As Wall (2010, p. 176) writes, 'ethical responsibility is not a capability installed in children that they otherwise lack. It does not appear at some magical age of reason. Rather, it is integral to human thinking throughout life.'

So, determining moral – or ethical – responsibility on the basis of age is, at best, arbitrary and often misleading. Very young children may not be able to make well-reasoned moral choices, but Chapters 5–7 indicate that the roots of how children learn to act and interact are established early in life. Moral education is a gradual process and one which both should, and does, take place right from the start.

Think of when a child is excluded from a game. This may not seem within the domain of ethics if others do not intend to upset the excluded child. But, as discussed in Chapter 6, even very young children are often more aware of the impact of their actions than adults think. It is often unclear as to what extent young children can recognize the likely, or possible, consequences of their choices. However, adults expect even very young children to think of these; and are rarely impressed by the cry 'I didn't mean to', except in the case of a total accident. The distinction between intentional and habitual conduct is more blurred, and that between thoughtlessness and malice less clear, than may appear on the surface.

One key task is to help young children to develop greater sensitivity towards other people and recognize the impact of their actions, even when this is difficult given their age or psychological development. As Gutmann (1987, p. 62) writes, 'moral education begins by winning the battle against amoralism and egoism'. Specific actions and behaviours matter, but the prior task is for children to recognize that they do not inhabit a morally neutral universe where 'anything goes'. Adults should not disclaim responsibility for moral education, broadly conceived, if children are to realize that how they – and other people – act and interact matters. The question is how best to help children learn, and act upon, this.

A common lament is that, without a definite code of rules, morality easily becomes relativist – with no solid basis, so that 'anything goes'. Those serious about ethics must be aware of the danger of relativism – where how one acts becomes just a matter of personal preference, what one might call a pick'n'mix approach. While this is a danger in a culture which emphasizes individualism and personal choice, in Holloway's (2004, p. 159) words, 'moral struggles are frequently between competing goods, rather than between a straight good and a straight evil. But that does not mean that anything goes.'

An old African saying states that it takes a whole village to raise a child. Much of any child's education, particularly in respect of attitudes and beliefs, takes place at home and in places other than school – such as places of worship and sports clubs and in informal interactions with friends and others where they live. As Noddings (2013, p. 171) reminds us, 'moral education is . . . a community-wide enterprise and not a task exclusively for home, church or school.' So, all adults who work with children should see their role in some respects as moral educators, though some will have a specific role. Parents/carers have a central, but not an exclusive, place in this process, with others, whether members of the extended family or local communities, teachers or those in other pastoral roles, sharing the responsibility. But we must not equate moral education with schooling, or see school as the only, or even the main, place where children learn how to act and interact.

The language used to describe moral education is no less tricky than that related to morality. Terms such as character education and values education are often used loosely with meanings that vary and are not always clear, often based on how these have been developed and described, and the role of religion, in different countries.

McLaughlin and Halstead (1999, pp. 136–8) identify two main strands in moral education, which they call non-expansive and expansive. The former emphasizes:

- a set of core, or universal, values;
- a specific programme to introduce and reinforce them; and
- a process of values being internalized more by repetition and habit than by conscious reasoning, at least with young children.

An expansive view highlights that values:

- vary between cultures;
- are internalized more through the hidden curriculum and modelling than direct instruction; and
- often conflict, so that children need to learn from a young age how to resolve such conflict by moral reasoning.

Halstead (1996, pp. 9–11) describes three main ways of approaching what he calls values education:

- character education;
- values clarification; and
- moral reasoning.

Character education as developed by Lickona (1992) involves trying to identify and then instil appropriate values, but Halstead identifies two main problems: how to identify which values are appropriate and ensure a consistent approach and how to deal with conflicting messages from outside school. Values clarification is concerned with how children explore and develop their own feelings and values, but has been criticized for encouraging relativism. The moral reasoning approach focuses on discussion about moral dilemmas, and is described and critiqued later in this chapter.

Halstead reported that, in both the United States and the United Kingdom, eclectic approaches were favoured. I shall argue for an approach which is eclectic, but not based on a discrete programme, recognizing that, for something as complex as moral education, there are many routes and any approach must take account of the context.

I suggest that moral education is best understood in two related senses:

- a broader one, related to the moral dimension running through all aspects of life and children's upbringing;
- a narrower one, of how children learn to act and interact appropriately and ethically,

a distinction reflected in the title of Halstead and Taylor's book *Values in Education and Education in Values* (1996). This distinction raises complex questions, which will keep recurring throughout this book and do not lend themselves to simple answers, among them:

- how young children learn both in general and in terms of ethics, and the factors which influence this;
- what 'appropriately' means; and
- how these two senses of moral education are linked.

The moral dimension is integral to education, rather than some branch of it such as mathematics or history, and must take account of aims, what education is for, rather than focus primarily on techniques. Opportunities for moral education, in both senses, exist in every interaction between adult and child.

I shall suggest that moral education, in its narrower sense, is more about actions than content, about procedural than propositional knowledge – more like learning to ride a bicycle or to swim than memorizing a list of spellings or the countries of the world. What helps children to become more compassionate and thoughtful towards other people falls within the scope of moral education; involving everyday, often apparently minor, matters such as whether, and how, to welcome a newcomer or respond to someone in difficulty. Such an approach is reflected in McLaughlin and Halstead's (1999, p. 136) words: 'all conceptions of "character education" (emphasise) a duty not merely to teach children *about* character (and virtue more generally) but also to *develop* qualities of character and virtue.'

Moral education is a long, slow process of which any individual parent or teacher, group or school is only a part. All those with whom a young child interacts affect how they learn. We must recognize the limits of what we can do. We cannot control how children will turn out, though we may influence, steer and guide. We can lay foundations, but not create the whole building – and must be aware of several pitfalls.

Pitfalls to avoid, dilemmas to address

What children learn is not necessarily what adults intend, especially in areas related to attitudes and beliefs. Any of several potential pitfalls may render efforts to influence how children conduct themselves unsuccessful and even prove counter-productive, particularly in the long term. This section identifies pitfalls to be avoided and dilemmas to be faced, whatever approach is adopted.

Apart from the belief that there is only one way to 'do moral education', five other potential pitfalls are:

- nostalgia
- hypocrisy
- indoctrination
- being seen as puritanical and a killjoy
- detaching ethics from real life.

Nostalgia has been common to older generations throughout history, partic-ularly in relation to morality. This reflects, and leads to, the view that in the past everything was better and that the morals of the younger generation are in decline; and is often linked to moral panic. Nostalgia is usually based on a highly selective view of what society was like, and the adults involved actually did, when they were younger. Such nostalgia is generally misplaced and, even if not, children are unlikely to take much notice of those adults who express it.

If adults do not 'walk the talk' – do what they tell others to do – even very young children soon spot hypocrisy and a lack of authenticity. One danger of this is that children may come not only to ignore a specific message, such as respecting those with whom one disagrees, but believe that morality itself does not matter, that 'anything goes'.

Indoctrination is a term with pejorative connotations, of exercising undue influence. However, most adults wish to exercise influence; and some may, reasonably, see their role as 'in-doctrination' in the sense of deepening a child's understanding of, and involvement in, a faith community. Adults exert considerable influence on, and power over, young children. The issue is, therefore, one of whether influence is undue, and power is misused. Indoctrination tends to make children reject other associated aspects of a religious faith or a particular moral stance, when they come, often in adolescence, to question specific elements. So, indoctrination runs the risk of creating a brittle sense of moral identity. Moreover, the fear of being accused of indoctrination may lead teachers, especially, to avoid controversial but important issues.

Most children want to do what they enjoy and are likely to complain when this is forbidden without good reason. Being (or being seen as) puritanical and a killjoy can easily lead to children seeing morality as restrictive – about what they should not do – rather than enabling – what they should – denying them opportunities to do what they enjoy. Ethics is best presented in positive terms, using subtle means of influence, rather than moralizing and preaching.

Detaching ethics from real-life situations is a pitfall more likely when moral education is seen as a mainly cerebral process. Young children benefit from examples related to, or drawn from, their own experience to illustrate the link between their actions and the more abstract language of ethics, if they are to see how the latter relates to their own lives.

Three more contentious potential pitfalls to which teachers may be particularly prone are:

- believing that adults have all the answers;
- being punitive towards children who behave inappropriately and/or their parents/carers; and
- relying on discrete programmes.

Wall (2010, p. 170) writes: 'the notion that moral education applies primarily to children allows adults the comfort of feeling that they have reached some plateau of moral certainty. But this feeling is a dangerous one.' Adults may be better at reasoning about what they should do, but do not seem necessarily to act better – whether this means kindly, compassionately or altruistically – than children. We should be wary of believing that we, as adults, cannot learn from children, or that moral education is always a one-way, adult-to-child process.

Children's inappropriate behaviour, particularly towards other people, is often disruptive; tending to provoke adults to blame the child, if s/he is thought capable of controlling his conduct, and parents/carers – or both. Such a response is hard to avoid. Adults must seek to understand and care for, rather than blame, children and create relationships of trust, especially for those with least experience of these. Parents/carers have a vital role in moral education, but some may be unable to fulfil it well, or have a different view, however legitimate, of how their child should be brought up. Such differences are often related, uncomfortably, to issues of class, religion and ethnicity. But messages which are broadly consistent across different parts of their lives help children to conduct themselves appropriately. So, parents/carers and teachers must try to work together, in ways discussed in Chapter 10, rather than blame each other.

Educational policy, and character education, have tended to emphasize discrete, often short-term, programmes. However, I shall argue that such programmes are unlikely to be successful in the long term unless part of an approach embodied in how individual adults act and settings operate, rather than 'bolted on' or adopted in only a few subject areas.

This discussion starts to expose various underlying dilemmas, with no easy answer. The first relates to the basis of morality – why one should act in any specific way and expect children to do so. For many people in the past, and still, morality has been rooted in a religion. Since the Enlightenment, and particularly with the decline of attendance at organized worship, the basis of morality has frequently been different, for instance what leads to happiness or human rights. Moral educators, particularly outside the home, face a dilemma about the extent to which their approach should be based on a specific view of morality – and if so what this should be – and to what extent take account of the child's – and family's – background. Most groups will include children brought up at varying points of a spectrum running, broadly, from 'You can do as you like' to 'Do as I tell you', where at one end there is little guidance or structure and at the other very clear prescription. This dilemma is more acute in diverse societies and groups and is discussed in more detail in Chapter 2.

A second dilemma is the extent to which adults should provide clear, simple messages about how to behave. The 'common sense' view is that young children need these. Sometimes, they do. But uncertainty and the fear of relativism tends to encourage adults to offer over-simple messages, often presented as rules to be applied regardless of the situation. To disregard differences of background and culture may cause some children or their families to feel uneasy, offended or excluded. Moreover, oversimplification may result in children being poorly equipped to cope with the question of 'How should I act when I am not sure?' In real situations, this usually entails balancing different imperatives. Explicit, non-negotiable messages may help some children, particuarly those least sure of what is expected. But I argue for a more nuanced approach, where children, from an early age, are encouraged and helped to engage with, rather than avoid, complexity and to learn to exercise judgement depending on the situation.

A third dilemma is whether adults should treat all children the same. 'Of course, that's only fair', you may be tempted to answer. But it may be appropriate to respond in different ways to two children who make a similar comment, depending on judgements about the children's age, background, intention and other factors. Such an approach may be seen as unfair; and the start of a slippery slope which makes excuses for children not taking responsibility for their own actions. Chapters 7 and 8 consider the dilemma of consistency in more detail.

A rather different dilemma is to what extent adults should present morality as related primarily to the individual's actions and interactions, or to bigger societal issues, such as climate change or world poverty, whether war is justified or how to counter injustice. This dilemma can be harder for (at least) two reasons. First, such issues often make us, adults or children, feel powerless because they are so huge and hard to change, leading to worthy but superficial responses. Second, adults, especially teachers, may be forced into taking a strong stance for or against a particular position, and so run the risk of exerting undue influence and possibly accusations of indoctrination. In my view, while young children should increasingly be encouraged to consider such issues, and how individual actions and social structures are linked, the main focus of character education should be on what children can do in their everyday lives.

These dilemmas indicate the importance of context, beliefs and judgement. It is all very well for someone (like me) to say what a parent or teacher should do, in general terms. The actual process of deciding what to do is in practice almost always messier and begs more basic questions. The approach of someone who believes that moral education involves ensuring that a child avoids certain actions deemed to be wrong or remains a member of a faith community will vary from that of someone who believes that children should learn to exercise their critical judgement in such matters. If an adult is uncertain how, or indeed whether, to try and influence a child's actions and shape her character, this is bound to affect what he does. However, the more serious danger is not to recognize the influence that adults exert, like it or not. Giving the message that 'anything goes' is to abdicate this responsibility.

Recent debates on young children's moral development

Two contrasting views of moral development have been influential in the last forty years:

- the cognitive developmental approach, associated with Lawrence Kolhberg (1981, 1987); and
- that of feminists such as Carol Gilligan (1982) and Nel Noddings (2003, 2013) who emphasize relationships and care.

Key points are discussed clearly in Winston (1998, pp. 13–24) and Russell (2007, pp. 23–49) and summarized in this section.

Kohlberg's work is based on a view of children's development similar to that of Piaget, best known for his ideas on cognitive development, although he also wrote (1932) on moral development. Piaget saw development as a growing ability to understand and follow rules, with these initially given by external authority and gradually internalized. Kohlberg presents moral development as a series of consecutive, linear stages, where a child moves from one to the next; rather like climbing a ladder, with a definite end- or high-point. He identified six stages, divided into three levels, as indicated in Table 1.1.

Kohlberg assessed an individual's stage largely on reasoning about abstract moral dilemmas, what one would do in situations such as whether it is right to steal drugs to save one's impoverished but sick parents or to kill, or be an accomplice in the death of, someone who no longer wishes to live. He presented moral development as the ability to make increasingly rational and autonomous judgements about right and wrong, emphasizing abstract reasoning and principles based on justice, valid regardless of culture or context.

The clarity of Kohlberg's model is intuitively appealing, with children moving from simple, concrete motivations to complex, abstract ones. Chapter 6 considers some limitations of a Piagetian model of development, especially in relation to attitudes and beliefs. But let us note that Vygotsky (1978)

Table 1.1 Kohlberg's levels and stages of moral development

Level 1 Preconventional morality	Right and wrong determined by rewards/ punishment	Stage 1: Obedience and punishment orientation (*How can I avoid punishment?*)
		Stage 2: Self-interest orientation (*What's in it for me?*)
Level 2 Conventional morality	Views of others matter. Avoidance of blame, seeking approval	Stage 3: Interpersonal accord and conformity (*Social norms, the good boy/girl attitude*)
		Stage 4: Authority and social-order maintaining orientation (*Law and order morality*)
Level 3 Post-conventional morality	Abstract notions of justice. Rights of others can override obedience to laws/rule	Stage 5: Social contract orientation (*Recognition that rules should sometimes be broken*)
		Stage 6: Universal ethical principles (*Principled conscience*)

emphasized learning as a social task, where children's conceptual development is supported by those with more experience. Although primarily related to cognition, such a view indicates that children require the support and guidance of others. Development, whether in ethics or otherwise, does not happen 'naturally' without assistance.

The cognitive-developmental approach tends to rely on answers about how one would respond to profound moral dilemmas. Few of us ever have to make such decisions; and if one does, the context may override what seemed right in theory. Most of ethics is more mundane, like what sort of activities to participate in or avoid, whether to visit a lonely friend and how much to give to charity. For young children, ethics relates mostly to areas such as being kind to others, telling the truth and respecting other people's property – and when and how to do so.

Kohlberg's model was challenged by Gilligan (1982) on both methodological grounds and a fundamental disagreement about the basis of morality. She pointed out that Kohlberg's empirical work was done exclusively with boys and men. Moreover, she questioned the assumptions implicit in most Western, male thought that everyone (broadly) proceeds through similar stages towards the end-point of autonomous, rational choice. Gilligan suggested that women tend to see morality more in terms of context and relationships, often asking for more information and not seeing the 'right' solution as reached solely by reasoning. Relationships and compassion may matter more than justice and principle. Gilligan argues that reaching the highest of Kohlberg's stages is almost impossible for those who take account of the context.

Noddings builds on Gilligan's call for an 'ethic of care', presenting feeling or sentiment as the foundation of morality, with one vital source 'the memories of and longing for caring and being cared for' (2013, p. 149). Noddings calls for caring to be 'the foundation – and not a mere manifestation – of . . . morality' (2013, p. 42); and for ethics to be understood in group rather than just individual terms, a communitarian rather than an individualistic view.

Noddings writes of the ethical ideal involving an interdependence between the 'one-caring' and the 'one-cared-for'. Noddings (2013, p. 53) sees caring as 'a genuine response to the perceived need of others'. She points out that each person (of whatever age and status) is at different times the one-caring and the cared-for, and benefits from this, as 'the one-caring and the cared-for are reciprocally dependent' (2013, p. 58). So, the foundations of ethical action lie in reciprocal relationships, rather than individual, rational choice. The 'one-cared-for' gains, but the 'one-caring' is enriched by so doing. Noddings sees 'caring-for' as a stronger, more intimate feeling than 'caring-about'. So, we may care about the victims of natural disasters or conserving the environment, but caring for involves a more personal response and relationship. However, Noddings argues that prior experience may result in what she calls 'a diminished ethical ideal'. So, those unused to being cared-for will find it harder to be the 'one-caring' and a child who has been abused is likely to find it harder to 'care-for' than one who has experienced loving, supportive relationships.

One should not be starry-eyed about young children and how they can act. Anyone who has read Lord of the Flies or seen how a group of 8-year-olds can systematically make a child's life a misery will realize how unkind children can be. But, as Wall (2010, p. 24) indicates, 'children and adults are vulnerable both within and without, within to their own less-than-good tendencies, and without to the destructiveness of the world'. We are, in Noddings' (2013, p. 6) words, 'dependent on each other even in the quest for personal goodness'; and 'it is precisely because the tendency to treat each other well is so fragile that we must strive so consistently to care' (2013, p. 99). People – of whatever age – will not act ethically as long as they are focused primarily on themselves, so must recognize the needs of others. We must take personal responsibility for our actions, but some collective responsibility for each other.

Wall (2010) identifies three main views of morality and how they see childhood:

- the top-down, associated with Plato, Augustine and Kant, where children are seen as unruly and to be tamed with discipline imposed;
- the bottom-up, that of Rousseau, where children are regarded as innocent, with gifts to be drawn out; and
- the developmental, linked with Aristotle, where children start as ethically neutral, but are defined largely in terms of what they lack.

Noddings (2013, p. 96) comments that Kohlberg provides 'only a hierarchical description of moral reasoning, not a model for moral education'. Wall argues for a radical rethinking of what ethics involves, based on respect for children, challenging the Kohlbergian model of rational, adult men as 'kings of the moral castle'. He sees relations as central to ethics and children engaged in, and contributing to, this right from the start, stating (2010, p. 179) 'from birth onwards, moral life is an endless re-making of relations'. Placing children centre stage helps to show our mutual interdependence. Ethics must address how we treat each other, particularly those who are vulnerable, as we all are at times. For Wall (2010, p. 170), 'moral education is not the stage-specific unfolding of increasing capabilities but the initiation of selves into socially ordered virtues and character'.

This chapter has pointed to the complexity of the landscape of moral education, pitfalls to avoid and dilemmas to address. You may see me as straying beyond the boundaries of what can sensibly be called moral or underplaying the role of religion or clear rules. I shall try to justify and elaborate my views in the subsequent chapters. In Chapter 2, we consider the basis of ethics and will see that this is no less complex.

2

The Basis of Ethics

Why act in any particular way?

Let us start by thinking of reasons a child (or any of us, though adults may be better at hiding the real reasons) might give for acting in a particular way. Some examples are given in Table 2.1. The empty spaces indicate that there are many others.

Such a list raises several issues, the most obvious of which is any of us – child or adult – act as we do, for many reasons including:

- reward and punishment
- rules
- competition
- self-interest
- greed
- fear
- shame
- compassion
- altruism
- duty

- pleasing others who care for us
- paying back, either as revenge or gratitude
    and that sometimes we don't really know.

Some reasons in Table 2.1 seem to be linked to morality or ethics, others, especially those on the bottom row, not. For instance, 'I couldn't help it' denies personal responsibility and 'I wouldn't get caught' is a pragmatic reason, in contrast to ideas such as fear, conscience or altruism.

Usually, we have mixed motives. So, I may visit a friend in hospital, out of compassion, because I would feel good if I go or ashamed if not, even self-interest in that he may support me when I am in difficulty. A child may ask another to play to make a new friend, out of kindness at seeing someone lonely, or because an adult may commend or reward her for doing so.

Suppose that a 6-year-old has taken another child's toy. Most people would think that he should be expected to own up. But on what basis? That it is wrong to steal, it harms someone else or not doing so will make him feel guilty and unhappy? Or that he is a kind child who has done something he now regrets?

What if a 10-year-old is bullied on account of her skin colour? Should the perpetrators be persuaded to change their behaviour on the grounds that it is unfair or uncaring? That it will lead to unhappiness for both the child

Table 2.1 Possible reasons a child might give for his or her actions

My mum or dad told me to	The rules say I should	It is what God wants me to do		I wanted to see how an adult would respond
It is the sort of action I think is right	That's how someone I admire acts	I wanted to do better than last time	I wanted to do better than someone else	
It would make me happy		I would feel ashamed if not	Someone was kind to me	It would make my friend happy
I would get told off otherwise	I would get a sticker	I would be beaten up otherwise	I was scared of being left out	I wanted to get my own back
I couldn't help it	My friend told me to	I don't know	I can do what I want	I wouldn't get caught

bullied and those doing the bullying? That it is not what one would expect of those individuals, or how people act in that school? Or simply that it is against the school rules?

In practice, adults may appeal to any of these or indeed a combination. As we shall see, emotion plays a more immediate and stronger role than cognition in our responses, particularly for young children and those under stress. Young children are often focused on their own needs and only gradually learn to regulate their emotions. So, their actions tend to be based more on emotion than deliberation, and inappropriate actions are often impulsive or thoughtless, rather than malicious or unkind. 'I don't know' may be an attempt under pressure to duck responsibility, but young children often have not thought about, or be able to work out, the possible consequences. This is not to excuse unkind behaviour, but young children often need help to think through the consequences of their actions, and be supported in doing so with increasing compassion and sophistication. The nature of such support must take account of the child's emotional state and the extent to which s/he can make considered decisions.

Ethics involves actions based on thinking of others rather just oneself. So, the type of motivation matters. Being motivated to act in a particular way usually requires an incentive, especially when doing so is not immediately in line with one's instincts and desires. Extrinsic motivation involves acting with a view to gaining some reward or avoiding punishment or sanction. Intrinsically motivated actions may bring less tangible rewards, for example feeling good or gaining the approval of others, but this is not the prime reason for one's action.

As discussed in Chapter 6, young children are often motivated by factors different from those which motivate adults or which many adults assume will motivate children. While extrinsic motivators may be useful in the short term, ethical action needs, increasingly, to be based on intrinsic motivation. To develop intrinsic motivation, children must recognize why their actions matter rather than the reasons seeming imposed or arbitrary.

Young children often find it hard to regulate their actions, know why they have acted as they have and understand the impact on other people. So, an appeal to fairness may be too abstract for those determined not to miss out, and one to kindness ineffective, especially for those with low levels of empathy. Ethics is not just about 'knowing', rationally, how one should act. The gap between knowing and doing is far wider than that between knowing and not knowing.

Case study – walking the talk?

One afternoon, I was teaching an unfamiliar class of 8-year-olds. A group had been out that morning to present to a conference how class discussion helped them make decisions about how to behave. I saw one girl from that group, jostled by another child, look round to check that no one was watching and then deliberately kick his ankle really hard. When I challenged her, and pointed out the mismatch between what she had been saying in the morning and how she had just acted, she looked scornful, suggesting, without saying so, that she saw little connection and did not see why I should.

This story illustrates that children often act differently from how they say they will, or should, act – just as adults do. The girl seemed to lack intrinsic motivation, wanted to get her own back and thought that she would not get caught. How would one start to assess her stage of moral development? Ethics involves 'walking the talk', not just reasoning what one should do or parroting what one has been taught.

One puzzling aspect of ethics is the place of altruism, acting in a way one believes to be right even when to do so may not (seem to) be in one's best interests. For example, ignoring a stranger in trouble is usually likely to be safer than helping, but even so it is usually regarded as better to help. The appeal of self-interest remains strong in all of us. It may be ultimately in our best interests to act cooperatively, for instance in giving blood or working as a group, but it is usually not obvious why anyone should act other than out of self-interest, although plenty of people do act altruistically. While even young children do so at times, it is unsurprising if often they act on the basis of what will benefit themselves. The same is, after all, true of most adults. Conscience acts, for many adults, as a brake on self-interest. However, Chapter 6 discusses how emotions which rely on cognition, such as conscience, do not develop beyond a simple level until middle childhood; and public shaming, if linked to identity, is usually counter-productive.

So, motivation is rarely simple and often based on emotion rather than reason and influenced by both external and internal factors. We must also take account of cultural differences. Rogoff (1990) shows how adult expectations, and how children respond, vary significantly between cultures. In some, children are expected to learn primarily by watching, listening and doing, in others by asking questions and thinking. In some societies, children are expected to defer to their elders, in others encouraged to make their own decisions. In some, a religious code provides a framework for how to behave, while in others expectations have a different basis. For instance, many South Asian cultures emphasize *izzat*, roughly translated as family honour, which involves acting modestly and avoiding behaviour which contravenes socially accepted norms: a view at odds with many of the assumptions common in Western society. How intrinsic motivation is built, over time, for different children from varying backgrounds, is the conundrum.

Relying on rules, religion or rights?

The rest of this chapter discusses three main ethical traditions – duty ethics, virtue ethics and utilitarianism – and how these relate to religion and rights as the basis of ethics, particularly in working with young children. First, let me say a few words about traditions. Traditions tend to be associated with an unchanging, even ossified, view, taking little account of changing circumstances. So, for instance, many people see religious traditions as inflexible, particularly about morality. Although traditions can be like this, Macintyre (1999, p. 222) writes that 'traditions, when vital, embody continuities of conflict', with Winston indicating that 'Macintyre understands a tradition as a living argument, not a set of precepts to enforce conformity' (1998, p. 21).

Tacey (2004, p. 153) points out that 'to refuse to dialogue with tradition is a sign of continued youthfulness and adolescence, and a denial of the deep sources that nourish us'. Traditions encapsulate the wisdom (as well as the prejudice) of previous generations. To take no account of them is to cut ourselves off from this wisdom. So these three traditions provide a source of guidance, but should be approached critically.

Put simply, duty ethics sees morality primarily as about questions of right and wrong, with a code of rules requiring little or no interpretation to determine which course of action one should adopt. In virtue ethics, the emphasis is on the sort of person one should be or become to live a good life. Utilitarianism emphasizes happiness, and the happiness of the greatest number of people.

We shall discuss each of these further. But first let us note that Haidt (2012, pp. 116–20) highlights three different bases for ethics – those of autonomy, community and divinity. The first sees people, first and foremost, as individuals with wants, needs and preferences, the second as primarily members of larger entities from families up to nations. The ethic of divinity is based on the idea, hard to understand for those without religious beliefs, that people are children of God and should act accordingly. These may seem irreconcilable, but I believe that, in a diverse society, one must strive towards an approach to ethics with young children which can be adapted but act as a foundation for different systems of morality, both religious and secular.

Most adults in Western societies base their view of morality – and moral education – on duty ethics, with rules to indicate how one should act. The code of rules may be drawn from sources such as law, religion or human rights or be more locally determined, as in a family, a group or a school. For instance, religious codes such as the Ten Commandments or precepts in the Quran rely on a source such as a holy text or a person with religious authority. However, duty ethics is also associated with the Enlightenment, notably the philosopher Kant, who argued that reason can, and should, be used to work out the correct course of action, based on universally applicable principles such as justice. The cognitive-developmental approach described in the previous chapter is strongly influenced by duty ethics.

Ethics as the application of rules presents an easily comprehensible and simple framework, providing clear boundaries, which has a strong intuitive appeal for those working with young children. Most settings display expectations of how children should behave, usually in the form of rules to enable the smooth running of the group. These are intended both to encourage compliance with social norms and to offer ethical guidance, although the boundary between these is often blurred. For instance, 'we are kind to each other' or 'do not take someone's property without asking' are designed both to maintain order and encourage ethical conduct.

Clear, inflexible rules may be helpful, especially for those who are confused, in black and white situations, like whether one should 'hit back'. However, such rules work less well in more complex situations. In real life, most ethical decisions are not simple 'either-or' choices, because so much depends on context. Nussbaum (2001, p. 30) argues that, in relation to moral claims, 'what we find in practice is not a sharp contrast between absolute claims and claims that can be avoided with ease but a messier continuum of claims judged to have various degrees of force and inevitability'. The danger of relying too much on simple solutions is that they easily infantilize children and leave them, as they grow older, poorly equipped to cope with the mixed messages about how to act and interact they are bound to encounter.

The emphasis on rules in duty ethics should not be seen simplistically as one or more rules may pull in different directions, highlighting the need for judgement. Even very young children must be encouraged, and helped, to exercise discernment. However, the binary nature of duty ethics – that an action is either right or wrong – risks taking too little account of context and the impact on other people.

Morality has historically been strongly linked with religion. Religion provides for many people a detailed moral framework, for others a broad basis, even when individually they are not members of any faith group. For other people, morality is in no way dependent on religious belief or affiliation. Religion has often underpinned the legal system, which provides a structure to deal with more specific issues, for instance how disputes and crimes should be addressed and the individuals involved should be treated. Such a structure may be explicitly religious, as in many Islamic societies, or more residual in societies in Western Europe based on Judaeo-Christian principles, even though religious affiliation is no longer widespread. But the great 'meta-narratives', such as religion, offering definitive answers to fundamental questions, however attractive to some, no longer work for many people in a fragmented world.

Most religious traditions present a view of how life should be lived, both prescribing and proscribing, some 'do's and 'don't's. Christians are taught that love of God, and other people, should be the basis for how their life should be lived; and Muslims are expected to live in accordance with Quranic principles and practices.

While religion is often associated with codes which provide little scope for individual discernment and choice, this is not always so. The Ten Commandments offer a more inflexible code than the New Testament injunction to 'love one's neighbour as oneself'. Judaism has detailed codes to help determine what is permissible and otherwise, but the interpretation of these may be the subject of endless argument. Within Islam, *sharia* law, often seen as inflexible, provides five categories, broadly translated as:

- obligatory
- recommended
- permitted
- discouraged, and
- forbidden

Only the first and last give no scope for human judgement, while the middle three provide guidance but allow scope for human decision.

Religious belief is sometimes claimed to be a necessary basis of ethics, with the reduced influence of religion is often linked to moral decline. However, such a claim is increasingly hard to sustain for two main reasons:

- while religion motivates many people to good works, often at considerable personal cost, it has also led to many actions which would be widely condemned. Indisputably, many people act well on a basis other than religion; and
- there are many coherent bases for ethics, such as human rights, which are not dependent on any religion, even where some of the language and thinking draws from religious traditions.

This said, Putman and Campbell's research (see Arthur, 2010, p. 93) in the United States suggested that Christians are better citizens than others in the sense of giving more to charity and volunteering. However, they concluded that it is not a particular theology that predicts good citizenship, but the extent to which believers are embedded in a network of religious friends. Which groups one belongs to really matters; and may matter more in relation to morality than belief.

Religious affiliation has, especially in much of Europe, become both less common and more varied, as societies have become increasingly diverse and secularized. As a result, many children have no religious affiliation and know very little about religious traditions, or ethical codes associated with them. Even so, we should remember that, for many children, religious faith, often linked to cultural expectations, is the framework for how they have been taught to act. So, the argument that ethics *must* be based in religion seems unsustainable. However, an inclusive and widely applicable approach will take account of, but not assume, religious affiliation, but not depend on religion as the basis of ethics.

Morality has increasingly been based on secular or humanistic principles since the Enlightenment. The United Nations Convention on the Rights of the Child (UNCRC), adopted in 1989, emphasizes universal rights for all children, such as those to life, survival and development, not be discriminated against, their views to be respected and their best interests to be considered in all matters affecting them. Article 12, for instance, states 'every child has the right to have a say in all matters affecting them, and to have their views taken seriously.'

While some children's rights seem unconditional, such as those to life, some seem to be conditional in that children will require (at least some) adult help to exercise them. For example, very young children have a right to be heard, but their wishes may need to be mediated by adults, since they may not yet be able to make decisions likely to benefit themselves – or others – in the long term. However, Wall (2010) sees the discourse of human rights as systematically excluding children, while recognizing (p. 123) that the UNCRC is a step forward in adding participation rights to those related to provision and protection. He (2010, p. 89) writes: 'in a world structured around agency, individuality and autonomy, those who are relatively less independent in life will tend to be assumed, however benignly, to be second-class moral citizens.' Wall regards Kohlberg's work as 'inherently biased precisely against children. For at each stage, children are chiefly defined in terms of what they lack; first a sense of wider community, then a capacity for impartial reasoning' (2010, p. 80).

Wall's work raises the question of to what extent children – we all – develop morally. Your immediate answer may be 'of course'. However, if one sees ethics in terms of actions rather than rationalizations, it is far from obvious that moral development occurs in the same way – or as smoothly – as physical or intellectual development; or that adults act more selflessly, kindly or honestly than children. Indeed, they very often act more self-interestedly, for many reasons, among them status, power and greed; and adults may have much to learn from children.

The final section of this chapter considers some of the difficulties with an emphasis on religion, rules and rights, particularly with young children; but now we discuss virtue ethics.

Living a good life?

Macintyre (1999) draws from a tradition in Ancient Greece, notably Aristotle, to argue that the fundamental ethical question informing correct actions are 'how should I lead my life?' and 'what sort of person should I be/become?' rather than Kant's 'what rules ought I to follow?'; and that the question of 'what makes a person virtuous?' should come before 'what makes a decision right or wrong?' This tradition, virtue ethics, emphasizes the attributes, or virtues, required for 'a good life' or a life well-lived. Later in this section, we consider different conceptions of a good life, though, obviously, not in the sense of eating and drinking to excess.

Virtue ethics sees ethics as not just a set of separate, individual decisions, but considers people as whole persons, members of groups with responsibilities towards each other. A range of interlinked virtues contribute to a person's character, over time, influencing both consciously and otherwise how one acts. Although, unfortunately, the Ancient Greeks' emphasis was solely on men and indeed on citizens, virtue ethics can be applied to anyone.

In Ancient Greece, virtue was intimately associated with one's place in the *polis*, the city, or society, so that ethics was not just a matter of individual choice, but how to conduct oneself appropriately in a social, as well as an individual, context. Aristotle does not see moral agents as solitary individuals but members of interrelated communities involved in a common life (see Russell, 2007, p. 56). Right action is not simply a matter of personal whim but involves a consideration of how our actions affect other people, whether those immediately around us, or on the other side of the world. So, what constitutes living well cannot be seen just in individual terms.

Virtue ethics encourages discernment about the right course of action, according to context. Virtue consists of finding the best course of action between two extremes. In Comte Sponville's rather florid language (quoted in West-Burnham and Huws Jones, 2007, p. 42): 'every virtue is a summit between two vices, a crest between two chasms: hence courage stands between cowardice and temerity, dignity between servility and selfishness, gentleness between anger and apathy.' In more child-friendly terms, doing what is right may involve being brave, but not so brave as to put oneself in danger; or being generous, but not to the extent of giving away all one's possessions. Finding the appropriate course of action usually involves what I call the Goldilocks approach, neither too much, nor too little.

The Ancient Greeks saw virtue in unitary terms, arguing that a virtuous man will exercise and exhibit virtues such as prudence, courage, temperance and generosity throughout his life. Such a view seems demonstrably inaccurate. Those who show generosity are not necessarily brave, nor those who demonstrate compassion prudent. The idea of a person being virtuous or vicious, as a whole, runs counter to the modern Western view that our character, or identity, is made up of a range of traits. Each person exhibits these to a different degree depending on the situation and may act in apparently contradictory, or uncharacteristic ways, at times. I may, for example, be generous with my time, but not my money, or courageous in the face of some challenges, but afraid to face up to others.

Virtues are attributes which we do, indeed should, exercise, as appropriate, depending on the situation, and are developed through practice. As Aristotle (1998) argued, we become generous by acting with generosity and brave by the exercise of courage, helping to explain how these attitudes and attributes become embedded and internalized.

Carr (2003, p. 231) writes that 'what may be especially plausible about virtue ethics is that it offers clear criteria or moral value and virtue that precisely cut across any and all culturally grounded normative differences . . . we can see that people from different parts of the world have very different – even contradictorily opposed – moral beliefs but we are nevertheless able to recognize certain cross-cultural criteria of moral attitude and conduct.' We consider the thorny question of which virtues one should cultivate in young children in Chapter 7.

Kristjansson (2013) challenges ten myths about virtue ethics, among them that it is religious, paternalistic, individualistic and entirely situation-specific. Depending on which virtues are prioritized, virtue ethics can be adapted for a religious or non-religious setting. We all require guidance on what constitutes appropriate conduct, but such guidance need not be paternalistic if open to discussion and debate. Virtue ethics does run the risks of individualism and relativism – that one can pick and choose which virtues to adopt and that the rightness of an action is not independent of a particular culture or historical time. To avoid the former, virtues must be seen in social terms rather than just a matter of personal choice. For virtue ethics to be situation-specific is a strength, if this encourages discernment; but this does not necessarily entail moral relativism in the sense that 'anything goes'.

Kristjansson articulates three misgivings about virtue ethics as the basis of moral education. The first is that virtue and character are hard to study empirically. I do not believe that one can know quantitatively the effectiveness of any approach to moral education at anything other than a simplistic level; but that does not stop one 'knowing' its effect more intuitively. The other two are that little is known about the impact of previous interventions and that the history of efforts at character education do not have a good track record. Kristjansson (2013, p. 282) indicates that 'endless flavour-of-the-month varieties' result in dismissive attitudes among teachers and 'initiative fatigue'. This provides a warning against discrete, possibly superficial, programmes, with moral education a 'bolt-on', rather than an argument against virtue ethics.

A single parent living with a large family on a run-down estate may have a very different view of what constitutes a good life from a wealthy executive travelling regularly around the world; as may a Hindu computer scientist aspiring to a successful career in the United States, a Buddhist monk living a solitary life of reflection and a Christian missionary working to relieve poverty in Africa. If based on religious faith, a good life may entail a strong element of compassion, charity or determination to share one's faith with others. If based on material comfort and possessions, qualities related to competitive individualism are likely to be given a high priority. So, what a good life involves, and the attributes required, will depend on factors such as culture, religion and beliefs.

For Aristotle the end of human life was to flourish, to live well, to lead a good life. He emphasized that the exercise of virtue is closely linked to *eudaimonia*. This word is often translated as happiness, but as Grayling (2001, p. 73) points out this loses the original 'strong, active connotation of *eudaimonia* as well-doing and well-being, as living flourishingly'. *Eudaimonia* was seen as a sustained, rather than episodic, state, distinguishing between immediate and long-term happiness. Gratification, or feeling good, may result from a range of stimuli, chemical, social or personal, possibly not linked to, or even militating against, longer-term flourishing. Indeed, the Ancient Greeks emphasized that *eudaimonia* should be independent of health, wealth or the ups and downs of everyday life. A good life, one truly worth living, leads to such a state of flourishing.

What constitutes children's well-being, and the factors which help to promote it, are complicated and varied. Maslow's hierarchy of needs (1970) indicates that all people have a range of basic needs such as freedom from hunger and pain and feeling safe, without which well-being is impossible. Many children's well-being is compromised by the social conditions in which they live, involving poverty and exclusion. Adults can only do so much to ameliorate this, but they can do something.

Some factors which help to promote well-being and protect children against mental health difficulties, such as engaging in physical activity and being alert to the world around, and its beauty, are not closely associated with ethics. But others like having secure, nurturing relationships with family and friends, being a member of a faith community and acting altruistically, are more so. Well-being depends, to a significant extent, on the emotional and relational context in which children grow up, indicating that well-being often follows from attending to, and helping, other people rather than to oneself or one's own happiness or material possessions. So, while it is natural for adults to want children to be happy, the next section discusses difficulties with happiness being considered the main aim of education and ethics.

Searching for happiness or meaning?

The belief that societies should be organized and one's life based on a search for happiness is one associated with the tradition of utilitarianism and maintains a strong appeal for many people. Utilitarianism says that society should seek to achieve the greatest happiness of the greatest number of people. Layard (2005) and Layard and Dunn (2009) argue that society should be organized to enable people to be happy, linking this to physical well-being and a reasonable standard of living. Layard recognizes that above a certain level additional wealth does not lead to greater happiness, which depends on other, less tangible, factors such as experiences and relationships. Wilkinson and Pickett (2009) indicate that happiness is not correlated with material comfort above an optimum level, but that there is a close correlation below that.

Noddings (2003, p. 1) argues for happiness to be a main aim of education, because almost everyone wishes to be happy and children (and adults) learn best when they are happy; and more specifically, in relation to ethics, 'happy people are rarely violent, mean or intentionally cruel' (ibid., p. 2). The appeal of happiness is often strong for young children and those who work with them. Children want to be happy – we all do – and many parents say 'I just want her to be happy', especially with very young children. There is strong evidence of an association between children's engagement in learning and sense of agency with being happy, or at least not unhappy. So, I am not against children being happy. To see, and enable, this gives me great joy, but serious problems arise with happiness being seen as an end in itself. These are discussed in Eaude (2009) and summarized briefly here.

The first is that children tend to equate happiness with gratification, for example through material possessions, rather than a more active sense of well-being, as described above. Conducting oneself appropriately often does not make one happy in the short term; and may be against one's own self-interest, even in the long term. The pursuit of short-term pleasure may be an obstacle to well-being, in the broader sense of thriving or flourishing. Making one's own happiness the rationale for action tends to lead children – and adults – towards self-obsession and narcissism, though the happiness of a group may be a more enriching and appropriate goal.

Second, while learning is often enjoyable, it also involves struggle and requires resilience, in ethics as in other areas of learning. An (over-)emphasis on happiness tends to underplay the difficulty of deciding how one should act – and can give young children an excuse, an escape from taking responsibility for their actions.

Third, happiness is often usually elusive if one strives for it directly. In Mill's (1909, p. 94) words, 'ask yourself whether you are happy and you cease to be so'. A deeper, long-term sense of well-being is usually a by-product of experiences and activities such as nurturing relationships, challenges overcome and helping other people by being compassionate, generous or altruistic.

Fourth, an emphasis on children's happiness tends to prompt adults to say that they will make better what in fact they can't. Adults have an understandable wish that children should be happy and a strong inclination to protect them and to say that everything will be alright, even when this cannot be guaranteed. Adults may avoid discussion of difficult matters such as loss, illness or death; or war, injustice and poverty, ostensibly because such issues are too hard or controversial for young children to deal with. Avoiding or giving definite answers to such questions helps to protect adults from what is painful, but it patronizes and misleads children. Yet, young children have to make sense of difficult and controversial issues, and be helped to do so, in ways appropriate to their age and development, if they are to develop sensitivity to, and empathy for, other people.

Most religious traditions are opposed to a utilitarian view, arguing rather that:

- this life is not the only or the most significant aspect of existence, but, in many religious traditions, a preparation for another;
- the value of each human life should not be measured; and
- individual happiness matters less than living a life based on love or justice, duty or virtue.

While religion is often associated with duty ethics, it can easily be reconciled with a virtue ethics approach.

Hull (2001, p. 171) writes, poignantly, discussing his becoming blind, 'the most important thing in life is not happiness but meaning'. Dewey's (1916, p. 236) words, 'the main effect of education (is) the achieving of a life of rich significance' may seem a rather grand aim in relation to young children. But we shall see that making sense of (often puzzling) experience is at the root of one's identity and that children are active searchers for meaning and identity, right from the start.

However attractive the certainty that a clear moral code offers, children need a more internalized, intrinsic basis for their actions and interactions. In Holloway's (2004, p. 33) words, 'command moralities may exercise a nostalgic appeal in a time of confusion . . . whatever other characteristics the emerging morality must have, it must be characterized by the principle of consent.' While the word 'consent' may be problematic when considering very young children, an approach which does not develop intrinsic motivation is unlikely to be successful in the long run.

As Wall suggests, adults should take more account of children's rights. However, two dangers need to be recognized. The first is practical. For young children – and others – an emphasis on rights is problematic unless they recognize that individual rights must be balanced with the collective responsibilities which come with living with other people. Otherwise, children will tend to focus on themselves, rather than their place in groups and responsibilities towards others.

The second danger is that an emphasis on rights can lead to a neglect of what actual children actually need. Noddings writes that care ethicists do 'not ignore or discount rights, but we believe that rights arise out of acknowledged needs. There are times when people do not want the rights that generous advocates would thrust on them; they want, instead, to have their expressed needs heard and acknowledged' (see Noddings, 2005, p. 148). Such a view is supported by Williams' (2000, pp. 92–3) insight that recognition, by others, of one's own humanity must precede, and underpin, any emphasis on individual rights and responsibilities.

The three traditions described above may seem rather abstract in relation to young children. None is free from risk but it may help to think of:

- duty ethics as involving rules which provide clear-cut solutions, but easily underplaying the need to develop and exercise judgement depending on the context;
- virtue ethics as developing attributes to be exercised depending on the situation, requiring discernment, but with the risk of relativism; and
- utilitarianism as seeing happiness as paramount, risking that short-term gratification will be mistaken for a deeper, more fulfilling sense of well-being.

This book explores how moral education, in both the broad and narrow sense, occurs and how adults can best enable it. To do this, I draw on:

- the insights of Wall and Noddings, in particular, to formulate a view of ethics based on relationships and care;
- the tradition of virtue ethics based on attributes and dispositions to lead a good life; and
- research into how children learn to provide a basis for how adults should enable this.

I try to describe a constructivist approach which:

- provides relatively simple messages for children, but encourages them to learn to act appropriately when faced with complex ethical decisions; and
- enables adults to engage with the messiness of real life as a parent/ carer or teacher but helps to avoid the pitfalls and resolve the dilemmas described above.

Such an approach must link what children actually, and should, do, in ways which can be developed with increasing sophistication.

I shall suggest that neither rules, whether religiously based or not, nor the search for happiness, provide a sound, long-term foundation for ethics. And that the basis should be one's moral identity – the sort of person one is and wishes to become – which can best be described, and sustained, by cultivating the attributes and dispositions associated with character and virtue, so contributing to a long-term sense of well-being, or *eudaimonia*.

Subsequent chapters explore how character and moral identity are created and sustained, with children as active participants but guided by adults. From this, I suggest that a virtue ethics approach, based on the attributes required to lead the good life provides the most promising way ahead. Before that, we consider the social and cultural context in which young children grow up.

3

The Changing Social and Cultural Context

Looking back fifty years

In Chapters 5 and 6, we shall see how background and upbringing helps to shape children's identity, even though identity continues to change throughout life. The culture and context in which we live exerts a strong influence on how we act and interact and our beliefs about how we should do so.

In this section, I describe briefly my own background and upbringing. This is partly so that readers can recognize influences on my thinking and reflect on those which affect theirs. But it also provides some insight into how different the social and cultural context was in my childhood, even in the UK, let alone in other cultures; and how young children now grow up in a more complex and confusing world.

Born in 1953, I was brought up in a middle-class family consisting of my parents, an elder brother and myself. We lived in a homogeneous, prosperous town not far from London. Most people were at least nominally Christian and very few were from an ethnic minority or spoke other than English as a first language. People with disabilities were very rarely seen. I was at private boarding, boys-only, schools from the age of 9, something which only a tiny minority of children did. It was a protected and privileged world.

I had a good memory and found passing exams relatively easy, going to Oxford University to study history. Most of the people I met were from privileged backgrounds. Uncertain what to do afterwards, I worked in a school for children with learning difficulties before training to become a primary school teacher. I taught children from 6 to 11 years old, first in a small suburban school, and then in a large new school with many displaced families. I became the headteacher in a multi-cultural, Church of England first school, in 1989. After nine years, I left that post to do a doctorate and then worked independently as an academic, and a writer, while continuing to teach young children and those who teach them. Among the books I have written was one on spiritual, moral, social and cultural development (Eaude, 2008a), though my views on moral development have changed somewhat since then, for instance with greater awareness of different traditions of ethics.

This brief account of personal and professional life may go some way towards explaining my interest in young children's moral education and how I present it in this book. However, what about more personal matters? So, a bit more detail.

I have lived alone for most of my adult life and have never married or had children, though have enjoyed a long-standing relationship, acting as a step-father to my partner's two children, but never taking the main responsibility for parenting. I have been fortunate to enjoy good health and not to experience serious difficulties or deprivation. So, I write as a white, middle-class man approaching retirement, with a reasonably wide experience of schools but not as a parent. Although not from a church-going family, I was a Christian for a while at university, and have an ongoing interest in questions associated with religion, but without being affiliated to a faith community.

These considerations provides more context and start to explain my identity – who I am, where I belong. But it says little of attitudes, of my character, what I am really like or the formative experiences and relationships which helped to create this. This is harder, because such questions become increasingly sensitive and individuals may either be unaware of, or not open about, their own qualities. Like most people, I do not remember many early formative experiences. But let me try.

As a child, home was not a place where other adults or children dropped in unannounced. I was generally happy with my own company, often going off on my own from the age of 8 or 9 to play in the recreation ground or to the local library. We did not have a television until I was about 9. Mobile phones, computers and the Internet had not been invented.

I always loved reading and history, the latter inspired by the stories told by, and the enthusiasm of, a teacher, Mr Owen, when I was 10 or 11 years old. I remember particularly my father taking me to historical sites – and the intimacy that such trips offered.

I was brought up with a definite code of expectations and expected to work hard, with an emphasis on academic subjects and play regarded as a distraction. At school, there was an underlying Christian ethos and a strong emphasis on sport. Corporal punishment, common in most schools a few years before, was used rarely. Somewhat solitary and anxious to conform and less interested in tangible rewards than adult approval, I was generally well-behaved, more through worry about being found out than other reasons. Like many boys, I was not encouraged to express my emotions, with shows of emotion seen as signs of weakness. I, and am still, wary about expressing my feelings openly, though I have tried to change this as an adult.

All these influences affect my identity, how I see myself as an adult. I have prized my independence, though in recent years increasingly recognize the importance of interdependence. While often keen to belong, I have always been a bit of an outsider and seen as rather serious and puritanical; and had relatively few close friends but a large circle of acquaintances. Although rather certain about what is right and wrong, in many respects, I have become less so in the last ten years.

I have never been particularly materialistic, nor interested in fashion or the latest technological gadgets; but am competitive, though more so in activities such as games, quizzes and sport than in my professional life. I have always been rather fearful of, and deferential towards, authority figures, even when (consciously) realizing that this is ridiculous.

One later formative experience which I remember occurred when as a 17-year-old I encountered, in a visit to a child's home, poverty in a way which affected me deeply. I could not believe that any one had to live in such terrible conditions. Working as a classteacher gave me a strong sense of the importance for young children of the relationship with teachers and other adults who care for them. And teaching those from less privileged backgrounds than my own opened my eyes to the difficult circumstances in which many children grow up. Subsequently, interactions with those from different cultures have altered my naïve assumption that my own worldview is shared by most people.

You may, by now, not be interested in this detail, or wanting to know more; or asking what this personal narrative has to do with moral education. Many of the themes will appear throughout the book, in the belief that culture, background and upbringing – and the adults involved in this – profoundly influence how children understand themselves and the world – right from the start; but that our identity – or more accurately identities – is always in a state of flux.

Exploring social and cultural change

Case study – different cultural assumptions

In my first term as a headteacher, two 8-year-old boys, good friends and good Muslims, kept falling out in a friendly way. Ajaz would complain that Imran had said that he 'drank beer', and vice versa. At first, I would say 'well, that doesn't really matter too much, does it?' But I came to realize that, to them, it did. A normal part of everyday life for me was to them a symbol of what was not only forbidden but a betrayal of their religious and cultural heritage.

The world in which I grew up was very different from that in which Imran and Ajaz, as children of Muslim parents who had migrated from Pakistan to England, were living. In this section, I describe social and cultural changes in my life time, especially in the UK, though many will be familiar in other countries and cultures. Some relate more obviously to morality, others less. These changes have combined to alter significantly the landscape in which children grow up, and parents, teachers and others associated with their upbringing must work. The process has been gradual and subtle, with elements which different people may see as beneficial or otherwise. This is like how a neighbourhood changes over several years, as old houses are knocked down or renovated, long-standing residents move out and new ones in, with the type of shops, of groups and of activities all changing. One may lament the passing of the old, or welcome the vibrancy of the new, and probably elements of each. Let us consider these changes before trying to analyse the impact on children.

Among key social and cultural changes in recent years which the Cambridge Primary Review (Alexander 2010, pp. 53–5) highlights are:

- changing patterns in both the immediate and extended family and communities;
- a much improved level of physical health, though greater concern about mental health;
- a higher level of disposable income and possessions for most but not all;
- a rapid change in types, and availability, of technology; and
- a less deferential approach to authority.

In addition, there has been in most industrialized countries a rapid decline in attendance at church, but a more varied pattern of religious affiliation. Being part of faith community has become less common for most children, but, for a substantial minority, religious affiliation remains a significant marker, and maker, of identity.

The last few decades have seen major changes in communities and neighbourhoods, most obviously but not exclusively in urban areas. There has been a substantial increase in the number of families where children do not live with both their birth parents or close to their extended family. Such a trend is, in part, related to higher rates of divorce and different patterns of adult relationships; and, in part, to greater geographical mobility, resulting from migration both between and within countries. So, communities exhibit greater ethnic, cultural and religious diversity as a result of factors such as the arrival of new groups and the pattern of many adults living greater distances from where they were brought up and their place of work. A variety of languages and ethnicities is much more in evidence than in my childhood, even in relatively monocultural communities.

Most children are physically healthier, despite recent concerns about obesity, attributed in part to a more sedentary lifestyle. Many diseases common when I was a boy are much less so, because of factors such as public health and vaccination campaigns and improved living conditions and nutrition. However, there is more concern about children's mental health, happiness and well-being in most industrialized countries, exemplified in reports such as Unicef (20007) and books such as Palmer (2006) and Layard and Dunn (2009).

The last thirty-five years has seen an increased standard of living for most people. For instance, while central heating, foreign holidays and dishwashers were rare in my youth, these are now commonplace. While most families are better off financially, childhood poverty remains at a high level; and there is greater inequality. Significant numbers of children grow up in conditions where:

- their home life is one where they experience many different factors which contribute to deprivation;
- there is little structure and routine in their lives; and
- their communities have a high incidence of violence and anti-social behaviour, for instance with gangs and illegal drugs being common.

In some cases, children may be in more than one of these categories. Any of these reasons mean that many children lead lives which are pressured and in some cases chaotic.

The rate of technological change has been very rapid. This has led to possibilities hardly imaginable fifty years ago, for example in medicine with the possibility of IVF, organ transplants or new treatments for disease. Computers and mobile phones provide a level of access to information, music and games hard to foresee twenty years ago, yet now taken for granted. Such activities play an increasingly important role in children's lives, where many spend several hours a day in front of a computer or TV screen, usually on their own.

Success has increasingly been presented in terms of material possessions and celebrity. What constitutes success has always varied depending on family and cultural background. For instance, in some families, such as mine, going to university was expected, in others, even now, beyond either parents' or children's dreams. In many families, boys were expected to follow in their father's footsteps; and the opportunities available to girls were far fewer than now. Now, advertising and TV suggest that success is equated with wealth and that the routes to fame and happiness are through good looks, sporting prowess or one-off events – to be like a model or a footballer, to do well in a talent show or win the lottery. Moreover, sophisticated advertising is increasingly aimed at children as consumers. In Wall's words, 'not only does the media create endless desires in children, just as in adults, but it also specifically targets children in order to create within them a "lifetime brand loyalty"'. (2010, p. 98).

Such trends are relatively easy to identify. Others are less so, and more a matter of opinion, especially those related to aspects as elusive as whether one should take notice of authority figures and whom one should emulate. In my childhood, people such as doctors, clergy or teachers were regarded – rightly or wrongly – as usually commanding automatic respect. Now, this is less common, for a variety of reasons, including the role of the media in exposing those who behave badly and the increased level of, and easy access to, information available, especially through the Internet.

These trends are associated with the expectation that individuals should have more choice, in areas from schools to shopping, medicine to media, and that this is always desirable, both for the individual and for society, and should be open to all. Such changes are often based on people being seen, and seeing themselves, as consumers, with the right to complain if the expected level of service is not met. This contrasts strongly with my childhood, where the range of choice was narrower; and only a minority of people expected such choice. As we shall see, these changes have brought many benefits, but some adverse consequences, especially those for whom choice is illusory and those least able to distinguish what will benefit them in the long term from what is superficially attractive.

Many structures, such as the family, including the extended family, community and religion, which provided (for better or worse) an ethical framework, are looser. Society is more individualistic, with greater emphasis on entertainment and being happy, often linked to material possessions and consumption.

Many of the changes outlined above have had profound and, in some cases, rapid effects. It would be strange not to welcome many of them, such as improved standards of health and nutrition; or to lament the lack of progress in reducing levels of poverty. Many may be beneficial in some ways and detrimental in others; and the effects are likely to be cumulative and to affect different children in varying ways. For instance, television has expanded children's horizons in terms of information, but encouraged a more sedentary lifestyle. Living in a culturally and ethnically diverse community has the potential to enrich children's knowledge of other cultures; but can also be difficult, especially for the victims of discrimination. But there seems little doubt that children now grow up in a more complex world with a range of stronger and subtler external influences than I did.

The next section explores how the changes outlined above impact on how children are seen, and see themselves. In trying to understand the implications for children's standards of behaviour and morals, one must be acutely aware of the dangers of nostalgia and over-generalization. Older generations have always tended to lament that moral standards have declined. These changes have led to a widespread fear among adults, particularly those with a religious faith, of relativism, which sees morality as largely a matter of taste or opinion, as in music or fashion; and the commonly heard belief that children will act in feral ways without discipline and a definite code of conduct.

When terrible events occur, such as the non-accidental death of a child, or riots such as those in English cities in 2011, there is talk of declining standards of morality, often resulting in 'moral panic'. The causes are often seen as family breakdown, the declining influence of religion, and lack of discipline; and linked to inadequate parenting, greater availability of drugs or increased levels of crime. Many of the incidents which give rise to concerns about the ethics of banking, the morality of phone-hacking or the disgraceful behaviour of public figures are more widely known only because of the encompassing gaze of the media. However, it is hard to know whether standards of morality either in society more widely or in relation to children have declined, or even how one would judge this. There is plenty of evidence of children and young people being selfish and violent in the past and thoughtful and responsible now; and of society being harsh and uncompassionate, and people being supportive and helpful, both previously and now.

I agree with White's argument (in Smith and Standish, 1997, p. 19) that 'the problem is not moral decline, but a certain *lack of confidence* about how we should behave and what we should believe'. This is the result of many factors, among them the strong, often conflicting, messages and pressures about how to act and interact, which affect young children especially because of their impressionability. So, we should be wary of moral panic, however attractive phrases like 'broken Britain' may be to headline writers.

Considering the impact on children

The Cambridge Primary Review (Alexander, 2010) argues that children grow up in a world which, compared to previous generations,

- is 'busier', so that they have less space, both physical and mental, to play in an unsupervised way, except through using technology and are, arguably, less used to concentrating for sustained periods of time, especially in groups;
- enables access to a wider range of opportunities, for instance music and sport, but usually under the supervision of adults, so that leisure and play are increasingly under adult control;

- emphasizes individualism, consumerism and, especially for girls, aspects such as sexualization and body image, providing mixed messages about what to aim for, and how to achieve it.

Palmer (2006) sees many Western societies today as characterized by what she calls 'toxic childhood', with adults giving less time and attention for children, more emphasis on children being entertained by video games and TV and consumerism and advertising promoting a view of success based on material possessions and other external factors. While Palmer's view may underplay the positive opportunities opened up, evidence such as that of UNICEF (2007) indicates that many concerns about children's well-being are well-founded. In many countries, what Gerhardt (2010) calls the selfish society has emerged. This does not mean that everyone is selfish but that there is strong pressure to act in selfish and narcissistic ways. A significant minority of both adults and children seem less aware, or immediately accepting of, the norms of behaviour in social situations, with the example set to some children that 'anything goes'.

As we shall see in subsequent chapters, a sense of agency, that one is, at least partly, in control of one's life, and the space and time to play, is fundamental to creating and sustaining a robust identity. Young children need opportunities both to relate to other people and to be alone, with adults enabling rather than overcontrolling. While, because of increased work or other commitments, parents complain about being too busy, they have also become more protective and risk-averse. So paradoxically, there is more opportunity for children to be on their own, but less for them to play independently outside the home. Mayall (2010, pp. 61–2) describes children's lives as increasingly scholarized, with more emphasis on school and school-related activities; and less on leisure and play. There is a danger, in Heath's (2010, p. 115) words, that 'childhood is becoming one prolonged stretch of spectatorship'.

Technology presents children, especially once into middle childhood, with new ways of forming and sustaining relationships, for instance through the Internet and social media. For all these, and many other, benefits, technology tends to:

- encourage instant responses and lead to the 'expectation of immediacy', where ways of being entertained are always readily available;
- distance the user from considering the needs of recipients, with the anonymity which comes from communicating through technology

making it easier and more likely for people to be more unkind than with face-to-face interaction.

Much of the diet of entertainment available seems to give little, if any, consideration to an ethical dimension. A culture in the media of a lack of respect for, and rudeness to others, is the norm. For instance, discourteous and offensive behaviour is often presented as a source of humour, with any complaint about this dismissed in terms that it was 'just a laugh' – and so implying that those making such complaints are overserious and self-righteous. The same is broadly true of concerns about the amount, and extent, of violence seen by children. Yet, Swing et al.'s (2010) study of 6–12-year-old children concluded that the time spent viewing television and playing video games are associated with increased attention problems. Anderson et al. (2010) conclude that exposure to violent video games is a causal risk factor for increased aggressive behaviour and for decreased empathy and prosocial behaviour. While one should be cautious of generalizing, a life dominated by technology seems to emphasize individualism and make it harder for at least some young children to develop the intimate, personal relationships they need to flourish.

For children, greater choice has presented fantastic opportunities, for instance in games to play, magazines to read and clothes to wear. But many young children may be ill-equipped to deal with such a range of choice; and many pressures, and the worries, usually associated with adolescence have increasingly come to influence younger children. The pressure to conform with one's peer group, wanting the most fashionable clothes or the latest mobile phone, has become stronger, and at an ever younger age. The emphasis on fashion and body image has led, especially for girls, to a greater and earlier awareness of sexualization. The cult of celebrity encourages children to adopt role models based on external rather than intrinsic qualities. The stability of middle childhood has been undermined by the pressure, stemming especially from advertising, to aspire to becoming someone different from who one is – inbuilding a feeling of dissatisfaction with who one is.

As Bruner (1996, p. 38) states, 'school, more than we have realized, competes with myriad forms of "anti-school" as a provider of agency, identity and self-esteem – no less at the middle-class suburban mall than on the ghetto streets'. The changes described above have opened children to being, and being seen as, consumers, emphasizing their own wishes, rather than taking account of other people's needs. Many adults, including me, have little idea of how much external markers such as the latest fashion item or most up-to-date gadget matter in how children's identity and self-esteem is created and maintained.

While many of these influences, seen separately, may seem harmless, they work in subtle and seductive ways. There is a danger of 'trivialization', which Hyde (2008) identifies, along with 'material pursuit', as one of two factors which inhibit children's spirituality. In my view, even more corrosive is the message that how individuals should act is largely a matter of personal preference, though paradoxically peer-group pressure has become stronger.

Williams (2012, p. 268) suggests that 'if we live in a milieu where a great many signals discourage empathy and self-scrutiny, and thus emotional awareness, we shall develop habits of self-absorption'. For children, particularly, such pressures lead to a greater emphasis on the self rather than the awareness of, and attention to, the needs of others essential to acting and interacting thoughtfully. As we saw in Chapter 2, Aristotle saw well-being, *eudaimonia*, as an active state of thriving, rather than simple gratification. However, the current emphasis on individualism and the pursuit of happiness (particularly through possessions) tends to result in the message that 'if you're good, you're probably a bit "sad", if you're happy, this is probably not because you are good'. The view of success and happiness as based on wealth and possessions underplays the importance of hard work and resilience.

Such influences affect all children, but in different ways. To generalize is risky, but the types of pressure vary significantly according to socioeconomic status. For instance, those from relatively affluent backgrounds may be more over-protected, more able to buy the latest fashion and more vocal about their possessions. Those from disadvantaged backgrounds are more likely to be *de facto* excluded and under the persistent stress which accompanies poverty and which, as Chapter 5 explains, makes self-regulation more difficult.

Families and formal settings such as schools help most children, but not all, to belong. For some, faith communities and voluntary groups provide this. But those who do not feel that they belong somewhere will look for somewhere else to belong. So, the incentive to present oneself in sexualized ways at a young age or keep company with those who get them into trouble may be strong for those children who are less secure about where they belong; and where adults are not present or those who are do not exercise control over this.

A combination of the social changes outlined above has resulted in less structure, in terms of family and voluntary groups, to provide guidance for children and adults being less willing, and confident, in doing so. As a result, many children receive mixed, confusing messages about how they should act, with these differing between, and often within, the home, the school, the local community and the wider culture – and less support in deciding how to act. Chapter 8 argues that an inclusive moral order in school provides the chance for all children to belong in an environment based on care and respect for each other.

The social and cultural context in which children grow up is very different from that of fifty years ago; and in many ways harder, particularly for those living in circumstances where the pressures are greatest. Young children now face a more complex and confusing world, as a result of greater social and cultural diversity, the breakdown of many traditional structures and the current emphasis on individualism and conceptions of success linked to consumption and celebrity. The next section discusses how children should be equipped for a future of constant change, suggesting that this should be based on cultivating deep-seated attributes, attitudes and dispositions to cope with uncertainty.

Preparing for an uncertain future

As Alexander (2010, p. 53) suggests, 'sometimes it must seem to children growing up in Britain today that they cannot win', as when their lives and enthusiasms are reported it is 'all too often in terms of stereotypes', appearing as 'suffering innocents . . . in a dark and menacing world' or 'little devils whose behaviour is out of control by adults'. It is less easy to believe in childhood as a time of innocence. Yet, as Cunningham (2006, p. 45) writes:

> children in the past have been assumed to have capabilities that we now rarely think that they have . . . So fixated are on giving our children a long and happy childhood that we downplay their abilities and their resilience. To think of children as potential victims in need of protection is a very modern outlook, and it probably does no one a service.

Hargreaves (2003, p. xi) highlights that the 'demands on young people and challenges facing them are vastly different from what they were' and that this is true also of the demands which they make. Children now grow up, for better or worse, in a world with fewer certainties than in my childhood and stronger, often conflicting, influences on their attitudes and actions, and mixed messages about how they should act. The world in twenty, let alone fifty, years is likely to change even more than between my childhood and now.

The pressures on children discussed in the previous section are unlikely to be reversed and will probably intensify. Globalization is likely to result in continued geographical mobility, leading to increasingly diverse communities, linguistically, culturally and religiously. Probably, fewer children will be based in secure families and local communities and more will grow up with multiple identities. Continued technological change seems certain, but in ways, at speeds and with consequences we can barely imagine, though information will surely become accessible with increasing speed and ease. Issues such as environmental degradation and climate change seem likely to matter more as their impact becomes more evident. Hargreaves (2003, p. 29) highlights that an increasingly globalized and fragmented society leads to greater insecurity. The world is likely to be one of more diversity, less consensus and greater anxiety.

Hargreaves (2003, p. xviii) describes what is often called the knowledge economy as really a learning society. He suggests that preparing children for this means that they will need 'a set of values, dispositions and senses of global responsibility that extend beyond the bounds of the knowledge economy' (2003, p. xix). Learning will increasingly not just be about memorizing information or acquiring skills, but being able to apply these in appropriate ways in unfamiliar situations. Being equipped for a changing world involves deep-seated qualities such as being flexible, inventive, resilient and a teamworker (see CBI, 2012). Some of these are general, like being able to think critically, debate and negotiate, which are essential to citizenship in a democratic and changing society. Others are more directly associated with ethics such as thoughtfulness, empathy and trustworthiness. Chapter 7 considers how these attributes come under the umbrella term, character.

The boundary between those attributes specifically related to ethics and others is far from clear. To illustrate this, consider what Claxton (2002) calls the 4Rs – reciprocity, resilience, resourcefulness and reflectiveness – as essential elements of what he calls 'building learning power'. While these are not distinctively moral, reciprocity is essential in caring for others and resilience is required to do what one believes to be right when other options seem more attractive; and both resourcefulness and reflectiveness are necessary in assessing which courses of action are most appropriate.

Claxton and Carr (2004), describing how to build up children's capacity to learn, emphasize strengthening valued responses to learning opportunities by:

- increasing their frequency and robustness;
- widening their domain; and
- deepening their complexity and competence.

They write (p. 87), 'we have tended to articulate these goals in terms of a combination of learning inclinations, sensitivities to occasion, and skills. We have described them as being ready, willing and able to engage profitably with learning.'

Claxton (2007) highlights *broadening, strengthening* and *deepening* learning dispositions, so that children apply them in an increasingly wide, unfamiliar and challenging range of situations, and using them with increasing depth and sophistication, even when the going gets tough. To enable this, learning environments must be what Claxton and Carr describe as potentiating, which

> not only invite the expression of certain dispositions, but actively 'stretch' them, and thus develop them. It is our view that potentiating environments involve frequent participation in shared activity . . . in which children or students take responsibility for directing those activities, as well as adults. (2004. pp. 91–2)

This view, while related to learning in general, is especially pertinent to how children learn to act and interact appropriately. It is not enough to be able to act in particular ways – such as being honest or acting thoughtfully towards others. Children must be ready and willing to do so, as well, in different situations and not only because of the fear of punishment or the promise of reward. Chapter 8 considers in more detail what a potentiating environment looks like.

Deakin Crick and Goldspink (2014, p. 29) argue that learning dispositions are intimately linked with identity or self-stories, and that these are articulated in the language with which students talk about themselves as learners. For young children especially, how adults help to reinforce children's sense of themselves as learners is particularly important.

Haydon suggests that what he calls values education should be seen as 'sustaining the ethical environment', 'the surrounding climate of ideas about how to live', observing that 'the ethical environment is always there; we cannot live outside of it' (2004, p. 118). He makes an analogy with the physical environment, suggesting that diversity is to be welcomed, similar to biodiversity in a healthy physical environment, 'a diversity among persons . . . with different points of view, different virtues, different commitments – even, perhaps, different prejudices' (2004, p. 125). Particularly in a world of diversity and rapid change, children must be equipped for what is unfamiliar and to experience, and learn to welcome, diversity.

While children – we all – are, understandably, most concerned with their immediate family and friendship group, the demands of a globalized society requires that people learn to understand those who are different; and to live with, and welcome, diversity. Putnam (2000) distinguishes between two types of capital – *bonding*, which helps groups to cohere, and *bridging*, which provides the glue across social and cultural divides. Children have to learn about both similarity and difference, what separates as well as what binds. Adults must seek to broaden children's cultural horizons and, particularly for older children, challenge simplistic assumptions and stereotypes. So, while young children naturally will bond first and most easily with those who are similar, as we all do, they need also increasingly to bridge with those who are different.

Adults have a strong and understandable wish to protect young children from harmful influences. However, the level of change and uncertainty means that children need, from an early age, to be equipped to steer a path through uncharted territory, rather relying on precise directions, bearings or GPS points to say exactly where to arrive or the route to get there. Like everyone else, children have to learn to live with contingency and complexity.

This chapter has suggested that social and cultural change has led to greater uncertainty about how to act and interact, with many of the traditional bases of morality and structures to support less available, rather than to moral breakdown or decline. Children are increasingly subject to strong influences and mixed messages, at an age when they may be least able to make conscious, considered choices. Such messages encourage obsession with the self, with individual happiness often presented as what to strive for and success mainly judged in terms of material possessions. Increasingly, children will need to be equipped with the attributes and dispositions to cope with a world of change and complexity. A complex, fragmented and changing society seems to make moral education increasingly important, though more difficult. Yet the moral dimension of all actions and interactions is often unrecognized, and many educators do not see moral education as their responsibility. To examine why, we must consider the current educational context and the challenges and opportunities this presents.

4

The Educational Context

Education as a moral practice

This chapter considers how policy and practice in education, or rather schooling, have affected the landscape in which teachers of young children work. However, this is relevant for other adults because the trends identified influence both adults' and children's assumptions about learning.

Education and morality have, traditionally, been closely linked. In the 1840s, the Home and Colonial Infant School Society saw

> the primary object of early education as being to cultivate religious principles and moral sentiments; to awaken the tender mind to a sense of its evil dispositions and habitual failings before it is become callous by its daily intercourse with vice. (Quoted in Lawson and Silver, 1973, p. 282)

While such a statement now seems outdated, or even offensive, Pring (2001) argues that education must not, indeed cannot, be value-free. Warnock (1996, p. 53) writes, 'teaching is an essentially moral transaction'; and Noddings (2013, p. 179) 'everything we do . . . as teachers, has moral overtones'.

Jackson, Boostrom and Hansen (1993, p. 277), while recognizing that teachers' freedom to act on what they believe and desire may be constrained by institutional and social forces, see teachers

> not simply as technicians who know how to run good discussions or teach encoding skills to beginning readers but as persons whose view of life, which includes all that goes on in classrooms, promises to be as influential in the long run as any of their technical skills.

Such a view is true not only of teachers – but also of parents/carers, priests and other adults – and whether their actions – and what they do *not* do – are for good or ill.

Most institutions – schools, religious groups or sports clubs – have an ethical strand to their work, so that they do not just teach the mechanics of reading, religion or rugby, but values, beliefs and attitudes. So, teaching reading is not just about performance in tests, religious education about affiliation to a set of beliefs and sport about winning; but also, one would hope, a love of reading, how to live one's life and how to win and lose graciously. Part of any adult's role when working with children should be to (try to) make them better people, whatever that may mean. In more academic language, education involves, and may be judged in terms of, both technical and ethical norms.

Education is not just about cognitive, academic development, but has much broader aims to do with the whole child. As Talbot and Tate write (Smith and Standish, 1997, pp. 1–2), 'which of us, after all, wants their child to leave school clutching a handful of certificates, but with no idea how to be a human being?' Such a view is recognized in legislation and policy. In England, successive Education Acts have required schools to provide a broad and balanced curriculum and have included spiritual, moral, social and cultural (SMSC) development (or a similar list) as a central aim of education. Inspectors must consider SMSC in judging the quality of education provided. Most schools include within their aims a statement which presents education more broadly than in academic terms, recognizing that spiritual, moral, social and cultural – and cognitive, emotional, physical, aesthetic and other categories – are not separate, but interlinked, dimensions of the whole person: an argument developed in Chapters 5–7.

Similar considerations apply in most other countries, though the emphasis on pastoral aspects and care tends to be much stronger with very young children. For example, Alexander (2000) describes how the Russian system makes much of *vospitanie* (upbringing, including a strong moral element). In the United States, such aspects are taught through civics, social studies and character education, since the teaching of religion is forbidden in schools under the Constitution. In Australia, Values Education was introduced widely from 2005 (see National Framework for Values Education in Australian Schools, 2005). In several Far Eastern systems, despite the emphasis on academic attainment, character education has a high priority. For instance, in China, teachers have a strong sense of moral purpose, despite a highly competitive academic system.

Education always has multiple and complex aims, inherently rooted in beliefs about what it means to be an educated person. Such beliefs are a matter of debate, with some people placing more emphasis on academic aspects, others more practical ones, or religion or character; or some focusing on individual attainment, others on skills associated with working together. As the Cambridge Primary Review (Alexander, 2010, especially chapter 12) suggests, the aims of primary education are multiple, contested and long term, a preparation for life rather just for schooling or employment.

Harold and Anne Berlak (1987, pp. 22–3) outline sixteen dilemmas, which they see as inherent in how any teacher acts. Some are to do with control:

- whether the child is considered 'as student' or as the 'whole child'; and
- who (the child or teacher) controls time, operations and standards.

A second set relate to the curriculum, whether:

- knowledge is seen as public or private, as related to content or process, and as given or problematic;
- learning is understood as individual or social, and as holistic or molecular (in small bits);
- the child is thought of as unique or having shared characteristics, as having individual needs or a common entitlement and as intrinsically or extrinsically motivated.

A third set are societal whether:

- childhood is seen as continuous or in different stages and whether cultural beliefs and practices should be seen as shared or in conflict;
- all children should be treated the same or allowances made for some, both in allocating resources and in applying rules.

While you may think that this overcomplicates teaching, Berlak and Berlak suggest that all teachers have to, and do, find what they call 'patterns of resolution' to these dilemmas, whether consciously or not. This is manifested in practice by the emphasis given to 'the basics' or other subjects, to creativity or conformity, to freedom or control – and many more.

In Alexander's (1995, p. 67) words, 'teaching is essentially a series of compromises', highlighting that dilemmas and choices cannot be avoided. Teachers have to find an optimal resolution for each dilemma; for instance, deciding how much time to allocate to particular groups, and which ones, and how much to set definite expectations and to allow children to exercise their own judgement or creativity. But they also have to balance different dilemmas. So, in responding to a child who has misbehaved, the teacher makes judgements based not only on policies and procedures, but also on factors such as her understanding of the child's background, the impact on other children and the particular situation. Where it may be appropriate to issue a public reprimand in some cases, a quiet word may be best in others; and how the teacher responds to the same individual in different situations may, rightly, vary. As discussed in Eaude (2012), the primary classteacher's expertise depends on being able to balance and resolve many dilemmas and tensions to meet multiple, often-conflicting aims.

Policymakers face similar dilemmas, though they work on a wider canvas and policy provides a framework to limit the extent to which patterns of resolution are a matter of individual choice. For instance, the emphasis on 'standards' and on behaviour management in the last twenty years have been designed to shape what is expected of both children and teachers – and have done so.

The rationale of many policies is related to the perceived benefit to society and social justice; and so these are framed, in part, in moral terms, with the desired outcomes usually assumed as uncontentious. For example, education in most countries has been seen as a key mechanism for greater equity and social mobility. The National Curriculum, and the Common Core, and the move towards inclusion, are based on notions of entitlement and breaking the cycle of disadvantage. These were designed to try and remedy the considerable disparity in the opportunities available to children and standards of attainment, especially in reading, writing and mathematics. Many policies have been explicitly designed to improve opportunities and outcomes for children disadvantaged by factors such as socioeconomic deprivation or speaking English as an additional language. Fullan (2003a) argues that part of the 'moral imperative of school leadership' is to contribute to a wider system which helps to reduce disadvantage. However, such apparently uncontentious views are problematic for three reasons.

First, morality is not simply a matter of intention. Any action, or a policy, must be judged by what happens as a result. One would not accept from a 7-year-old the explanation for a foolish but harmful action, that 'I didn't mean to', since he would be expected to take account of possible consequences. The impact of any policy is almost always multidimensional; and different policies may pull in different directions. So, planning and evaluating policy requires attention to both intentions and outcomes.

Second, since the aims of education are complex, what is emphasized cannot be reduced to what can be measured without threatening those aspects not open to measurement. Among these are spiritual, moral, social and cultural development, indeed many of the most important aspects of our lives.

Third, education is concerned both with developing individuals and with creating a particular sort of society. Since aims vary, how to meet these will inevitably be a matter of debate. This is true of questions of how reading should be taught and how much time should be allocated to the arts; and even more so for personal and contentious issues such as those to do with morality and ethics. Education is not just a question of 'what works', an idea discussed below; and moral education is intimately linked with aims and the sorts of people and society to be encouraged.

So, neither the rationale for policy nor its consequences are as simple as it may seem. For example, inspection was designed not only to judge school effectiveness but to encourage and enable parental choice and its outcomes have aroused fierce controversy. Rather than entering here into such debates, I simply observe that policy, however well-intentioned, often has broader, sometimes unforeseen, consequences.

Pring (2001, p. 102) argues that educational practice should '(bring) together a wider range of activities which embody the values and the moral aims which they are intended to promote'. The aims of education, and how these are to be achieved, must be aligned, as far as possible; but, as Pring indicates, the recent trends of policy have led to the actual practice of education becoming detached from a moral perspective, 'with no driving and unifying ideal, no coherent set of values' (p. 102). The next two sections discuss how this has been manifested in relation to young children, and the underlying assumptions.

Recent trends in educational policy and practice

This section summarizes the main international trends in, and rationale for, policy and practice in education in the last two decades. While most of the examples are drawn from an English context, similar trends are evident in many other countries.

One trend following the UNESCO Salamanca Declaration of 1994 has been towards inclusion, by placing more children with special educational needs and disabilities in mainstream schools. This policy was intended, at least in part, to enable such children to receive the same entitlement to education as others. The explicit moral intention is clear. However, inclusion has proved controversial both philosophically and practically. For example, inclusion may benefit some children included academically, potentially at the expense of others; but may also provide different types of benefit, for instance in able-bodied children learning to understand the needs of others. Including some children with special educational needs and disabilities may be in tension with the expectation on teachers and schools to maximize the numbers of those reaching a particular level of attainment in tests. Groups representing those with disabilities disagree on whether inclusion is appropriate, and for which disabilities; and many teachers are concerned about the level of resourcing and support available, even when they are philosophically in favour of inclusion. This example illustrates that the effect of one policy, however well-intentioned, is often mixed and that policies should not be seen in isolation.

The Cambridge Primary Review (Alexander, 2010, especially pp. 241–3) highlights the historic and continuing dominance of what it calls Curriculum 1 – English (or the main language of instruction), mathematics and sometimes science – and the lack of attention to the rest, Curriculum 2. This distinction has been reinforced in recent years in England by the designation of 'core' subjects in the National Curriculum, with these emphasized in formal assessment mechanisms, inspection and the timetable. In the United States, a similar emphasis on the Common Core is evident. In Australia, national testing has had a comparable influence. Young children's education has been increasingly dominated by a focus on performativity (Ball, 2003) and measurable attainment in tests in Curriculum 1. Anxiety permeates the system, based on a view that education is like a sprint race, rather than a long-term expedition.

The emphasis on performativity stems from a concern with league tables, both at national level in comparative studies such as PISA (Programme for International Student Assessment) and TIMSS (Trends in International Mathematics and Science Study); and locally in comparing results between schools and classes within a school. An obsession with grading has led to a worry about 'falling behind', as a country, school or individual. Frequent tests enable the performance of children and teachers to be closely monitored. Such an approach prioritizes the academic aspect of education, with a strong emphasis on 'standards' in a narrow range of subjects, especially reading and writing and calculation, and propositional, factual knowledge which can be tested relatively easily.

The result is, from an increasingly early age, an ever-greater focus on Curriculum 1, with reduced opportunities for the humanities and the arts, Curriculum 2, and for creative and practical activities. Few would argue that children should not learn to read, write and compute fluently. But the focus on Curriculum 1 and measurable outcomes has resulted in a separation, in practice, of the academic and affective aspects of learning, rather than seeing them as mutually reinforcing, like two intertwined strands of a rope.

This trend is reinforced by high-stakes assessment and inspection, focusing on measurable outcomes and checking that schools and teachers do likewise. Such a trend is often underpinned by parents being encouraged to judge schools and teachers by test results and, if they wish, to complain or choose another school. So, teachers and children focus more on what can, or will, be measured, at the expense of other, less tangible aspects. The result has been a focus on factual knowledge and content coverage, which in turn leads teachers to emphasize instruction, pace and compliance and discourages children from being creative, discursive and critical.

This emphasis has been accompanied by one on behaviour management exemplified in this story.

Case study – behaviour management

At the start of a day when I was teaching a new class of 9-year-olds I did not know well, Tom explained to me the procedures, if anyone misbehaved, starting with a warning, followed by 'time out', and involving the headteacher if need be. I thanked him but said to the class that I was sure with such a sensible group everyone would treat each other thoughtfully; and that I expected to notice people for what they had done well, rather than the reverse.

Behaviour policies tend to emphasize clear boundaries, consistency from adults and conformity from children. Even very young children are expected to exercise choice (and recognize the consequence of making wrong choices), with a widespread use of rewards such as stickers and smiley faces and of a graded level of sanctions. Often, this is backed up by a diet of constant praise. While such policies are often (at least in theory) agreed with the children and usually framed in positive terms, they reflect largely what adults expect, and are non-negotiable. As we shall see, such an approach to behaviour management may encourage compliance, but inhibit children from developing a sense of agency and ability to make independent choices.

A further trend in most countries has been an emphasis on the formal curriculum being organized by subjects and in small chunks, often with particular programmes designed to develop academic and social and emotional skills, some of which are discussed in Chapter 10.

Such policy trends are linked to a move towards manualization where both what is to be taught, and how, is closely prescribed. Manualization tends to:

- prescribe techniques;
- reduce the teacher's autonomy, with the expectation of what Sawyer (2004, p.13) calls 'scripted instruction' leaving little space for 'disciplined improvisation'; and
- underplay the centrality of the teacher's judgement, making the role more like that of an instructor who follows a set of instructions.

Behind these trends is the search for 'effectiveness' and 'what works'. Such ideas focus on methods rather than aims, discouraging consideration of the multiple and contested aims of education and emphasizing technical aspects at the expense of ethical ones. Yet 'what works' only make sense in relation to aims and what one seeks to achieve. Methods matter – and the final part of this book considers these – but without a clear view of aims, it is hard to see how one might achieve them. Moreover, some aims may be achieved at the expense of others. For example, if an intervention helps a child to pass an exam, but means that she becomes disengaged from studying that subject further, in what sense can it be said to have worked?

Particularly in relation to ethics, what works in controlling behaviour in the short term may not, in the longterm, encourage intrinsic motivation. So, a punishment for stealing may result in a child not repeating the action straightaway, but not change his motivation to steal, or result in greater attention to not being caught. The question of motivation and how it can be developed is considered in more depth in Chapter 6.

These policy trends have influenced profoundly how adults and children think. In many respects, they represent a 'top-down' approach, underpinned by assumptions which are often hidden and not universally shared. The next section considers these, questioning whether these policies and assumptions provide the best context for young children's moral education, whatever the intentions of those who devised them.

Underlying assumptions about young children and learning and teaching

In exploring the assumptions behind the policies discussed above, some explicit, others less so, the discussion moves into even more contentious territory. While many may seem like 'common sense' and have become widely accepted, I shall argue that these are not based on how young children learn best; and often lead to moral education, in the sense of learning to live well, being sidelined. This provides the basis for the argument that moral education for a changing world will need to adopt different assumptions and concentrate on aspects other than those currently in vogue.

The language adopted reveals many assumptions about learning. For example, the word 'standards' is widely used to refer to attainment in 'the basics', without recognizing the legitimate differences of opinion about what is 'basic' and 'standards' of what. A redefinition of what is meant by 'standards' or 'the basics' – to include, for instance, standards of conduct or consideration of other people's feelings as basic – might help to alter current priorities. The language of 'delivery' implies that knowledge is like a commodity which arrives in a box. The emphasis on instruction and outcomes tends to presuppose that education is largely about factual knowledge. In Eaude (2011, pp. 62–5), I argue for knowledge to be seen as propositional, procedural and personal/interpersonal: put simply of facts, processes and people. Deep learning – of the type really to embed learning – involves a combination of all these types of knowledge.

To illustrate this, think what planning a garden requires. One needs factual knowledge about the types of plant which thrive in that soil and when and where best to plant them. But procedural knowledge of how best to plant, water and nurture them is also required and, no less important, one must understand who the garden is for and how these people would like it to look and be used.

To take an example more closely associated with ethics, a group of children deciding how best to address bullying might need to think what bullying involves, how it might be addressed and how everyone involved could be encouraged to help prevent it. In this case, rules might be seen as propositional, how to implement these as procedural and how to engage the whole group as personal/interpersonal knowledge.

The search for 'what works' assumes that the aims of education are simple and can be largely taken for granted. Currently, aims are not open to real debate: improved test scores in 'the basics', preparation for secondary school and the (supposed) demands of working life. Aims have been simplified to reflect what can be easily measured, leading to the ethical dimension of education being overlooked in favour of the technical – 'doing things right' rather than 'doing the right things'. As a result, both adults and children have come increasingly to understand education in narrow terms, rather than a broader view of human fulfilment and well-being.

The emphasis on performativity results from, and helps to reinforce, an implicit assumption that young children really need only to know 'the basics' – and that an insistent focus on these is the best route to raise standards in these subjects. A narrow focus on literacy and numeracy implies that the arts and the humanities, and other more practical, experiential learning, are peripheral. Yet, Nussbaum (2010) suggests that the arts and the humanities are essential to a thriving democracy. And the Cambridge Primary Review (2010) argues powerfully for young children to have a broad and balanced range of experiences. In part, this is because to be an educated person requires a wide range of experience, activity and knowledge. But it is also because a broad and balanced diet helps to engage children's interests and so provides a better route to higher standards of literacy and numeracy than an insistent and narrow focus on Curriculum 1. Moreover, it helps to identify areas where children may have particular interests or talents – and to develop these.

Four largely unquestioned assumptions associated with testing and the trends described above are that:

- learning is linear and cumulative, as in mathematics;
- knowledge is learned in small pieces, rather than holistically;
- learning objectives and goals and targets are the best way to motivate children; and
- learning is mainly a question of individual performance.

In relation to ethics, these assumptions should at least be challenged. Otherwise, there is a danger of coming to believe that:

- ethics is like a subject rather than as a thread running through the whole curriculum and life, linked to, and influencing, all aspects of how a child thinks and acts;
- learning ethics occurs primarily by means of the teacher imparting knowledge to the child and the child striving to succeed on his or her own, on the basis of detailed, externally set targets;
- teaching ethics should be mostly a matter of instruction, with children just expected to listen and to behave well.

'Common sense' may suggest that instruction or a direct focus is the best way for children to learn. However, in Desforges' (1995, p. 129) words, 'direct instruction is . . . never, on its own, sufficient to ensure deeper understanding, problem solving or creativity'. And Katz (2003, p. 368) argues that 'when formal instruction is introduced too early, too intensely and too abstractly, the children may indeed learn the instructed knowledge and skills, but they may do so at the expense of the disposition to use them'. The obvious or direct route may not always be the best; and one's aims may often be met by indirect means. For instance, by focusing too hard on an academic outcome such as higher attainment in reading, or a more affective one like happiness, one may fail to achieve what was intended. Indeed, such an approach may even be counterproductive.

While testing individual progress may be necessary, in some respects, an overemphasis on this tends to assume, and promote the view, that learning is mainly about competition and individual performance rather than collaborative and social. Such a view flies in the face of much of the research discussed in the next three chapters on how young children learn, particularly in areas associated with character and ethics.

A further, largely unspoken, assumption is that approaches to teaching used with older children are appropriate for younger children. For instance, the formal curriculum and the timetable are organized on the basis of separate and discrete subjects, often in relatively short time slots. This is in contrast to curriculum models associated with the early years, based on the work of thinkers from Froebel to Montessori, who emphasized crossing subject boundaries and children having more control of how long they spend on activities. Recent changes have tended to mean that personal, social, emotional and moral aspects are timetabled as separate subject areas or programmes; and that there are fewer opportunities for sustained play and listening to stories, all aspects vital to how young children learn.

The focus on the formal curriculum has led to children's experiences and interests, especially those not related to school learning, being largely discounted. This is in contrast to traditions of young children's education, like those cited above, which emphasize the need to take account of the whole range of young children's experience, to engage their interest and to enable links between their learning in and out of school.

Another fundamental assumption of recent policy is that teachers, especially those working with young children, do not know best, and need to be shown, and to adopt, (relatively) simple ways of working. This is linked with the trend towards manualization, reducing the scope for teachers to exercise judgement. Ball (2003) argues that the emphasis on performativity requires teachers to organize themselves as a response to targets, indicators and evaluations; and to set aside personal beliefs and commitments. However, 'pupils will not learn to think for themselves if their teachers are expected to do as they are told' (Alexander, 2010, p. 308). Thinking for themselves is essential if children are to develop the deep learning required for motivation to be intrinsic.

So, current educational policy and practice is based on often-implicit assumptions about children, learning and teaching. Young children tend to be seen as 'empty vessels', to be filled, potentially disruptive forces to be controlled. Learning is seen as a race to be run, or a meal to be eaten in small portions, a serious business based on de-contextualized skills, to be assessed through measurement. And teaching is seen largely in terms of transferring propositional knowledge to the child, in ways externally prescribed.

This discussion highlights some underlying, often unquestioned, assumptions which reflect, and have led to, a lack of recognition of the multiple aims of education, a loss of breadth and balance and a lack of trust in teachers' judgement. These assumptions, while often taken for granted, are not the only ones possible. Indeed, much of the thinking underlying early years practice, and primary education in England in the 1970s and 1980s, relies on different assumptions. Subsequent chapters will consider whether different assumptions are needed, while recognizing the danger of misplaced nostalgia. For example, I shall argue that:

- young children should be seen as active creators of meaning and their learning as holistic, contextualized and often serendipitous; and
- teachers will require an extensive repertoire of teaching strategies, exercising judgement and discernment, since teaching inherently involves a series of dilemmas and compromises.

Implications for moral education

This section highlights some implications for moral education of the discussion so far. Moral education, as we have seen, can be understood in two rather different, though linked, ways:

- as a dimension of every aspect of education; and
- more narrowly as what enables one to live a good life.

The rhetoric of policy, for instance about standards, is that children's backgrounds should not be an excuse for low levels of attainment or for teachers not having high expectations. While it is hard to disagree in principle, this takes too little account of the difficulties many children face, as a result of the context in which they grow up. Children do not start on a level playing field. As indicated, the focus on standards and performativity has narrowed the curriculum and emphasized the academic at the expense of other, more practical types of learning and knowledge. This may be a disadvantage to those who find it hardest to engage with school learning and who most need a broad range of experiences to engage them. As Fullan (2003b, p. 69) writes, 'if test scores go up and engagement doesn't deepen, improvement will be superficial and unsustainable'. More fundamentally, West-Burnham and Huws Jones (2007, p. 89) argue that 'the system needs to get fairer not better; the focus on improvement may actually have worked against equity'. While such a conclusion is a matter of debate, this illustrates that what constitutes success is not simple. It may be that becoming fairer is an integral part of becoming better.

Let us consider two examples, broadly related to ethics, of how the assumptions discussed above may affect how moral educators work with young children. First, the dilemma about educating the 'whole' child or the child 'as student', comes sharply into focus when a teacher is expected to narrow the curriculum to improve test scores. Policy tends to be predicated on the assumption that the purpose of primary education is to enable good results in 'the basics', but most parents and teachers value a wider range of experiences, activities and outcomes, especially with very young children.

A second example is whether the emphasis on conformity and compliance and on external motivators to encourage good behaviour may militate against developing intrinsic motivation. Most children act thoughtfully and appropriately most of the time, look after each other and do not end up acting anti-socially. Therefore, you may think that the approach to behaviour management described above is successful, or even necessary. However, the assumptions are based on behaviourism, with an emphasis on habituation, supported by reward(s) and sanctions. Behaviour is not an independent entity, but always emerges out of a person's values, attitudes and beliefs about life and learning and the context in which they find themselves (see Deakin Crick and Goldspink, 2014, p. 29). The discussion in later chapters will suggest that other approaches are more likely to encourage intrinsic motivation; and that approaches may have to vary for different children.

The Teaching and Learning Research Programme (TLRP) (2006), a large-scale, cross-phase project, concluded that 'the conception of what is to be learned needs to be broadened beyond the notions of curricula and subjects associated with schools' and that 'more prominence needs to be given to the importance of learning relationships'. The first statement challenges the equation of education with schooling and the formal curriculum with what is necessarily most important. The second is particularly significant for young, and inexperienced, learners, for reasons discussed in Chapter 5. Relationships, reciprocity and learning processes are often overlooked in a climate which emphasizes performance, conformity and measurable outcomes.

We saw in Chapter 3 how the social and cultural context encourages children to focus on themselves, to see success in terms of material possessions and to seek immediate gratification. Moral education, in its narrower sense, involves challenging, and helping children to question, whether many of these are the route to well-being or should be the basis of how one should conduct oneself. Achieving a longer-term sense of well-being and fulfilment requires an emphasis on interdependence and service, rather than individualism and self-interest.

As we shall see, a range of learning mechanisms help to internalize the attributes which guide one's actions when acting autonomously; and, in the long term, actions are usually influenced more by beliefs and mindsets than by external factors. To resist external pressures to act in attractive but inappropriate ways, children need deeply embedded attributes associated with character and virtue. So, adults should focus more on cultivating these attributes and beliefs than on behaviour management and compliance.

Ethics involves acting thoughtfully in two senses: thinking of other people rather than just oneself and acting reflectively. Paradoxically, this entails acting 'unthinkingly' much of the time, and being able to reflect thoughtfully when necessary. This paradox is captured by Oakeshott's argument (see Erricker and Erricker, 2000, pp. 98–102) that there are two forms of moral life. The first:

> does not rely on the time, the opportunity or the inclination to reflect on the possibilities for action, but acts out of habit. It is neither rigid nor unstable, and its history is one of continuous change . . . It is learned by children just as they learn their native language, by being exposed to it every day, by imitation and thus by habit. (Erricker and Erricker, 2000, p. 98)

The second is

> one with which we might be more familiar, or at least would recognise as overtly 'moral'. This is characterised by 'the reflective application of a moral criterion'. (Oakeshott) claims that 'it appears in two common varieties: as the self-conscious pursuit of moral ideals, and as the reflective observance of moral rules.' (Ibid. p. 101)

While these two forms of the moral life are ideally mutually reinforcing, unconscious processes are fundamental, with conscious aspects only a relatively small part of this – the visible part of the largely submerged iceberg. This is illustrated by Haidt's (2012) metaphor of a sense of morality as like a rational rider on an intuitive elephant, with the rider nudging but the elephant largely in control of the direction.

The moral life, thought of like this, is a way of acting and thinking, to be 'lived from the inside'; just as becoming a scientist involves acting like a scientist, or a bricklayer as a bricklayer, rather than hoarding a store of knowledge about science or laying bricks – though that may help. What it means to live a good life is inherently more contested than what makes a good scientist or bricklayer. Learning to live well is more like learning to speak, swim or drive than remembering spellings or the names of kings and queens.

Take the analogy with learning to swim. The knowledge required is largely procedural – 'know how' – rather than propositional – 'know that'. In swimming, one may aim for safety, for speed, for style – and the demands of these may conflict with each other. And one may learn several different strokes. One learns to swim mainly by watching, by example, by actually swimming and by feedback, both one's own and that of a coach, rather than theorizing about swimming.

Propositional knowledge – information – and focusing on the detail may help those, but can get in the way, especially if this provokes anxiety in less confident or experienced learners. For instance, when learning to drive, I focused too much on the road and overcorrected until I could relax and see the bigger picture, not respond to every tiny movement. Becoming more confident and competent involved a growing body of 'case knowledge', a sense of how to respond in particular situations, on the basis of previous experience of similar situations.

Most children 'know', broadly, how to conduct themselves. Sometimes, they do not act as they should, but the challenge is to enable and encourage them to do so, initially with, increasingly without, adult support. Only a small minority are so confused that they do not know, broadly, how they should act and interact. Even with such children, the task for adults is not so much to tell as to show and to support.

This chapter has argued that education has a strong moral dimension; and that every educator's role includes a moral element, though not in the conventional sense of 'teaching right and wrong.' While recognizing that the underlying rationale of recent educational policy is at least partly moral, especially in seeking to create greater social justice, the emphasis on standards, performativity and effectiveness gives insufficient scope for the development of the whole child; and does too little to prepare young children for a world of diversity and constant change.

A coherent approach to educating young children must take more account, than at present, of the different dimensions of learning and the variety of ways in which they learn. And an inclusive approach to moral education, in its narrower sense, has to be:

- specific enough to identify attributes to be developed;
- broad enough to be inclusive of different views of morality; and
- adaptable to different settings.

Subsequent chapters will explore this in more detail, but first we consider distinctive aspects of how young children learn.

Part II

The Roots of Moral Development

Part I has argued that:

- the social and cultural context means that children grow up in a time of moral confusion and require the intrinsic motivation based on embedded attributes and dispositions to be able to act and interact appropriately in a time of change; and
- an inclusive approach to moral education, in its narrower sense, must be specific enough to identify what these attributes are and flexible enough to be applicable to those with different views of morality and religious and cultural backgrounds.
- the current educational context, in striving for academic results, takes too little account of the ethical dimension of education and the development of the whole child.

In Part III, we shall consider the role of adults, but first must explore how young children learn, right from the start, since, without understanding this, one cannot know how they learn in terms of morality and ethics. Chapters 5 and 6 consider what is distinctive about young children's learning, drawing especially from neuroscience and psychology, emphasizing how emotion and cognition are linked and how both internal and external factors affect the development of identity. Chapter 7 looks more specifically at issues related to ethics and character education.

As we shall see, much of what underpins how children learn to act and interact appropriately may not be closely associated with morality in the sense of distinguishing right from wrong. The roots of ethics, like those of a tree, are often tangled and intertwined. As with any structure, these foundations, though often invisible, are what provide strength, nourishment and security at times of difficulty and uncertainty.

5

How Young Children Learn

Lessons from neuroeducational research

In considering what can be learned from research about the brain, one must recognize that 'while neuroscience can provide valuable insights into learning, it is important to recognize its limitations. Educators should be cautious when transferring results from controlled laboratory settings to the complex classroom' (OECD, 2007, p. 148).

Second, as Blakemore and Frith (2005, p. 88) emphasize, 'one of the important lessons of brain research is that the behaviour that you see on the surface can have very different causes'. In particular, brain research seems to offer more robust evidence about cognition than emotion and about difficulties than normal brain function. So, one should be careful about claiming that 'hard science' provides conclusive proof and of believing popular but inaccurate neuromyths – claims supposedly based on 'brain science' but not supported by the research and therefore simplistic or, at times, positively misleading.

Third, while neuroscience can provide many insights, the mind is not the same as the brain, with other influences – especially those from culture and experience – affecting development throughout one's life. Neuroscience can only start to explain limited aspects of how mind, and character, develop.

Fourth, the evidence strongly suggests that the brain is plastic: that is it changes constantly throughout life and particularly during childhood. While early childhood has usually been assumed to be the most influential period, research (e.g. Blakemore and Frith, 2005, pp. 111–22) now emphasizes how the brain changes significantly during adolescence. So, early experience is influential, but one should be wary of extrapolating too far about the effects on later development.

While, as Geake (2009, p. 86) indicates, 'brain function rather than structure is the more relevant aspect for educational neuroscientific research', a little information about brain structure is needed.

A brief summary of brain structure and function

The adult brain contains some 100 billion brain cells, or neurons, each consisting of a cell body, to which dendrites and an axon are connected. These are connected to other neurons by synapses, creating complex neural networks. Early brain development involves the growth of the number of synapses and therefore connections. This process occurs at a faster rate among children than adults, but so does synaptic pruning, in which infrequently used connections are eliminated. So, the phrase 'use it or lose it' is largely accurate.

These connections enable electric signals to pass through the axons. But the process that allows signals to pass through the synapses depends on chemicals known as neurotransmitters. How different chemicals stimulate or inhibit learning mechanisms is very complicated, but their role emphasizes the importance of one's emotional state. Physical and emotional distress will dominate brain function unless alleviated. A high level of anxiety will lead to 'fight or flight' – aggression or withdrawal – making it harder to regulate one's behaviour consciously. Intense emotion interferes with how well conscious processes operate, and impairs working memory, especially in those who find it hard to regulate their emotions. While some level of stress helps the brain to function efficiently, frequent and prolonged stress alters the brain's inhibitory mechanisms and ability to regulate responses adversely. Regular patterns of activity, rest and sleep help not only in recuperation but in processes like consolidating learning in long-term memory.

(drawn mainly from TLRP, 2007)

Neuroimaging studies suggest that emotions and thoughts operate within different neural networks. Patten (2011) indicates that emotions involve many more brain systems than thoughts do and that emotions perform the first level of appraisal of incoming stimuli. Patten distinguishes between:

- *basic emotions* such as sadness, fear, anger, disgust and perhaps surprise which are largely innate and instinctive, not dependent on cognitive development for emergence nor on cognitive appraisal for their activation, and;
- *feelings* such as shame, guilt, jealousy and pride, which rely on a detailed analysis of incoming stimuli in relation to memory, knowledge and sense of self. These have a cognitive and cultural element and so need to be learned and are less well developed in young children.

As Geake (2009, p. 115) writes, 'the principle that emotions are critically involved in learning at a neural level supports the behavioural observations of teachers over the centuries. There is a bi-directional dependency: aspects of emotion rely on cognition and aspects of cognition rely on emotion.'

Evans (2001) indicates that until the rise of Romanticism, about 200 years ago, emotion and reason were not seen as at odds with each other, but mutually supportive. Only since then have we become so wary and distrustful of emotion and reliant on rationality.

While emotion and cognition are closely linked, emotion operates at a more immediate level, with conscious mechanisms helping one to regulate one's behaviour. Unconscious processes operate more quickly than conscious ones. Cognitive processes can usually, with maturity, override emotional ones. However, for young children (and adults at times of intense emotion) emotion is the stronger partner.

The structure of the brain is hierarchical, in that the brain stem develops first, with other areas such as the cortex developing throughout childhood and beyond. This helps to explain why some tasks are difficult, or impossible, for young children. For instance, Blakemore and Frith (2005, p. 145) indicate that performance in memory tests is linked to the development of the prefrontal cortex. The brain stem is crucial in processing emotion and, while the left hemisphere is mainly concerned with verbal and the right hemisphere with spatial processing, most learning requires the interaction of many areas of the brain. Clark (2006, p. 373) describes the brain as 'vast, parallel coalition of more-or-less influential forces whose . . . unfolding makes each of us into the thinking beings that we are'. Learning, in Goswami and Bryant's (2010, p. 163) words, 'depends on the development of multi-sensory networks of neurons distributed across the entire brain'. So, the idea of 'left and right brain' is too simplistic.

Goswami and Bryant (2010, pp. 142–4), providing an overview of brain function and the implications for the primary years, identify four main learning mechanisms:

- what they call 'statistical learning', in which neural networks are built, categorizing visual and auditory stimuli on the basis of similarities, an unconscious process which continues throughout life;
- imitation;
- analogy; and
- causal learning, where explanations and reasons are consciously worked out.

These learning mechanisms operate at all ages, though some conscious ones can do so efficiently only once the necessary brain structure has developed. For instance, being (consciously) self-reflexive about one's emotions helps regulate one's response; but such conscious mechanisms develop only gradually, and operate at only a fairly rudimentary level until middle childhood and work less well at times of intense emotion. This becomes particularly significant with very young children and those less used to, and capable of, self-regulation. However, a great deal of learning occurs through unconscious and automatic processes.

Goswami and Bryant (2010, p. 143) emphasize that 'social interaction plays a critical role in perceptual learning', continuing that verbal media-tion is not enough and that 'shared activity is required to mediate the child's acquisition, mastery and internalization of new content'. Donaldson (1992, p. 20) writes that:

> when we discuss the development of the human mind we are talking about processes of self- transformation: processes by which we turn ourselves into different beings. However . . . this is not a solitary effort. We are dependent in the most crucial ways on the help of others. And others may hinder or constrain us also. This is true from early infancy onwards.

Children – we all – construct explanatory systems to make sense of experi-ence. Representing experience helps to embed it in long-term memory. How experience is represented affects how efficiently this occurs. Representation is:

- first, and most profoundly, kinaesthetic, doing and enacting;
- then iconic, imitating, observing and drawing; and
- increasingly symbolic, especially through language (see Bruner, 2006, p. 23).

While adults can use all of these, very young children cannot and only gradually come to learn efficiently through language.

Bruner (1996, p. 79) observes that 'we seem to be more prone to acting our way into thinking than we are able to think our way explicitly into acting'. Throughout life, as Wall (2010, p. 75) states, 'embodiment is more primordial even than language'. While language becomes increasingly important, very young children learn primarily through actions and drawing rather than language. Even in middle childhood, and beyond, language remains a necessary but a limited tool for learning. This helps to explain why approaches based on discussion often have less impact on how children act than adults hope and expect. Chapter 9 considers the role of language in more detail.

Attachment, anxiety and agency

What, and how, we learn depends on many factors, some genetic, others linked to prior experience and the current situation. For instance, Kagan (1994) emphasizes the role of temperament, which seems to be largely inherited. Our actions are controlled to some extent by our genes and culture but some character traits seem to be natural, others learned or triggered by experience. Prior experience makes a considerable difference. So, a baby who has been ignored when she cries may cry more, or less, or respond differently as a result; and the same child will respond differently, when comfortable or comforted, from when wet or shouted at. For the purposes of parenting and teaching, the factors one can influence, and to what extent, are what matter most.

Think of a tiny baby. Her crying suggests how she is often overwhelmed by primal, biological needs. Babies are responding to sensation, emotion and external events, exploring what is part of themselves and what is separate and the range of puzzling sensations and experiences encountered. Their focus is, initially, on themselves and they are able only to explore within their own immediate environment, but they are, from the start, searchers for, and active participants in making, meaning. Research over the last fifty years suggests that babies are much more active learners than had been assumed previously, reflected in Bruner's words (1996, pp. 71–2) that infants 'were much smarter, more cognitively proactive rather than reactive, more attentive to the immediate social world around them, than had been previously suspected . . . they seemed to be in search of predictive stability from the start'.

Gerhardt (2004, especially chapter 1) indicates how a baby's development is affected by his or her upbringing. The prime carer, usually the mother, is vital in ensuring that those needs which the baby cannot meet unassisted – such as for nourishment, warmth and reassurance – are met. For instance, when the baby is hungry, most mothers are attuned to recognizing the need and responding appropriately. One key task in which babies and toddlers are engaged is learning to regulate their response to emotion in socially appropriate ways. Rogoff (1990, pp. 155–6) emphasizes how parents work with (and steer) infants' pre-existing focus of attention. The interaction between baby and adult through gazing, smiling, talking, touching – the list is endless – is how babies learn to make sense of experience.

Attachment theory stems from Bowlby's work (e.g. 1965) on how babies respond differently to potentially distressing experiences. Put simply, this suggests that babies develop internal working models which:

- are constructed as a response to anxiety during early infancy through the baby's relationship with the prime carer;
- influence how the baby regulates emotion; and
- strongly affect how babies act and interact with other people.

Models of attachment may be secure or insecure, with the latter usually divided into avoidant, anxious (or resistant) and disorganized. Children with secure models of attachment can cope better with adversity because they can access a 'secure base' which both provides emotional support and enables the child to be more adventurous and take more risks. Infants with avoidant models explore but take little notice of their mother and are not worried either at her departure or return, sometimes being more sociable with a stranger. Having learned not to rely on their mother in seeking comfort, they are less prone to express their emotions. Those with anxious models are reluctant to explore in their mother's presence and distressed when she leaves. Reunions lead to the baby trying to make contact but resisting the mother's moves to provide comfort, reacting either angrily or passively.

A small number of children with insecure attachments fit neither of these categories, showing both avoidant and anxious responses. Described as disorganized attachment, this leads to paradoxical behaviour, for example crying loudly but avoiding the mother's comfort, or approaching her without being able to seek comfort and support. Such children are thought to have strategies to seek the security they crave but be unable to implement them, having learned that these do not work predictably.

Reciprocal, predictable relationships, based on attunement to the baby's needs and responses, affect how babies learn to respond and regulate their behaviour. As children grow older, their need for the mother to be present diminishes, but that for anxiety to be contained remains. What may come relatively easily to a child used to predictable relationships and responses may be beyond those with disorganized models of attachment. Secure relationships and predictable responses matter most for those who have least experience of them. Yet, such children may be those who are most challenging. Those children who most need to be loved often search for love in the most unloving ways.

De Souza (2004, p. 62) writes that the elements that had nurtured the participants in her research 'in their sense of self, values and belonging, and in helping them find meaning and purpose in their lives, were clearly linked to the relationships they had formed from their very early years'. More generally, as Salzberger-Wittenberg et al. (1983, p. ix) suggest, 'our learning, in infancy and for a considerable period, takes place within a dependent relationship to another human being. It is the quality of the relationship which deeply influences the hopefulness required to remain curious and open to new experiences, the capacity to perceive connections and to discover their meaning.'

The relative importance of models of attachment and genetic factors and how permanent their effect is remains contentious (see Goldberg, 2000, p. 247). However, three main lessons emerge:

- how emotion is processed and patterns of behaviour are manifested depend (at least in part) on the internal working models, or models of attachment, learned in infancy;
- these result reciprocally from the types of interactions between baby and mother, with the mother's emotional attunement (broadly speaking, sensitivity to the baby's emotional state) key to enabling this; and
- anxiety continues to have a profound effect on children's responses and must be contained to avoid withdrawal or aggression and enable conscious mechanisms to operate.

Most conscious learning is based on attending to, selecting and resolving problems and doing so actively and constructively. This is described as agency – which, as Bruner (1996, p. 93) suggests, 'takes mind to be proactive, problem-oriented, attentionally focussed, selective, constructional, directed to ends'. A sense of agency involves being engaged by, often absorbed in, the activity or task in hand. Although the baby's attention span may be short, without engagement she will not actively make sense of her experiences.

Learning is, from the start, reciprocal and interactive, enhanced by responses which are predictable and attuned to the child's needs. While agency often requires individual effort, a sense of agency can also be collective. Just think how a parent talks to a 1- or 2-year-old, constantly pointing things out, naming them and encouraging the child to notice and respond; and how, gradually, the child learns to make sense of the world. While one can become over-engaged or over-focused, and much learning occurs without conscious thought, a sense of agency and engagement are vital, requiring that the child feel competent, capable and creative, and, at least to some extent, in control of the process, which in turn depends on feeling safe. As we shall see, a sense of agency is often constrained by the circumstances of people's lives and the consequent lack of power, particularly young children and those who are, or who feel, excluded.

Children – we all – need to be cared-for, most obviously when least able to meet our own needs. As discussed previously, Noddings (2013) argues that care for others is fundamental to ethics. Nussbaum (2010, p. 31) writes that weakness and neediness can create ethical deformation and cruel behaviour, unless narcissism and the tendency to dominate can be channelled in a more productive direction. External factors such as unpredictable early relationships and a threatening current context, particularly when combined, affect children's ability to make appropriate choices.

A lack of secure relationships in infancy and beyond may make caring for other people too risky and undermine a child's sense of agency. As a result, making choices is much harder for some children, especially when they are worried or fearful. This does not mean that adults should not expect children to act and interact appropriately. Far from it. But it does mean that some children require more support than others, especially to contain their anxiety; and that relying on conscious processes may be ineffective and, ultimately, reduce the child's sense of agency. Those children unused to secure and trusting relationships will need more nurture and less challenge and greater predictability and continuity of relationships. Early experience and current circumstances mean that children do not start from a 'level playing field'.

This section indicates that from infancy children are active learners, but need to be supported by predictable, caring relationships to help them deal with, and process, emotion appropriately. In Gerhardt's (2004, p. 24) words, 'unconsciously acquired, non-verbal patterns and expectations . . . are inscribed in the brain outside conscious awareness, in the period of infancy and . . . underpin our behaviour in relationships through life'. This helps to explain why some children are more, or less, resilient and able to regulate their responses than others; and highlights the continuing importance of unconscious processes and the limitation of relying on conscious ones.

Imitation, feedback and habit

This section discusses other learning mechanisms mentioned above, notably imitation, analogy and habituation and their link with feedback and role models.

One powerful, and subtle, way in which we, and especially young children, learn is through example and role models. As the playwright James Baldwin (1991, p. 60) says, 'children never have been very good at listening to their elders but they have never failed to imitate them'. Adults' actions tend to be more influential than what they say. Even very young children watch adults whom they trust closely and try to make sense of what they see. For example, recently, my step-daughter's son, aged two-and-a-half, asked why I was hitting his grandmother, when I gave her an affectionate pat.

We often underestimate the extent to which children pay attention to what adults do. I remember being approached, as a headteacher, by a mother who asked me to ensure that I wear a bike helmet. I protested that doing so was a nuisance, but she (rightly) insisted that if I did not it was much harder for parents to persuade their children to wear one. We are more important than we give ourselves credit for and what we do matters (far) more than what we say. Of course, children will not always respond as we hope; and with older children the effect of example may reduce as other, stronger, pressures exert their influence.

How imitative processes work remains a matter of debate. A body of research (such as Rizzolatti and Craighero, 2004 and Parker-Rees, 2007) suggests that mirror neurons may play a major role in human learning, as they do in monkeys. Mirror neurons are triggered both when an action is performed and when it is observed in another person. So, in Blakemore and Frith's (2005, p. 161) words, 'by observing an action, your brain has already prepared to copy it'. This may help to explain why young children often learn from observation more easily than from verbal descriptions.

However, whether mirror neurons even exist in humans remains a matter of controversy.

The psychoanalyst Lacan provides another explanation, writing about the mirror stage as a vital element in how identity is created. This is based on the belief that infants from the age of about six months recognize themselves in a mirror (or something similar) which encourages them to see themselves as an object that the child can view from outside himself. However, children do not begin to recognize that the images are reflections of their own bodies until the age of about 15–18 months. When the child becomes fascinated with her own reflection, she sees a coherent self, a self that is together and somehow integrated as one. But it is a sense of self at odds with her own internal incoherence and uncoordinated bodily functions. This discrepancy between the image and the subject is often resolved in favour of the image, which becomes a controlling source of how we think about who we are. Lacan came to consider this process not as a stage in the infant's life but as representing a permanent structure in how we come to see ourselves. We return to how identity is created in Chapter 6.

Seeing and copying other people's actions is a powerful way of learning. However, this is not like taking a photograph, but, like learning to speak, a reciprocal process, based on a cycle of modelling, practice and feedback. Young children tend to do more of what adults notice and to respond to more positive reinforcement from adults whom they trust, indicating the significance of adults modelling and reinforcing particular actions. While the harassed parent or teacher may often find this hard, a grandparent or teaching assistant may often be in a better position to do so.

Young children find it hard to engage with abstract ideas, out of context. Vygotsky (1978) argued that social precedes individual learning. Concepts are developed together before they are internalized, though such a process depends on activities and experiences being within the learner's Zone of Proximal Development, that is just beyond his or her current level of understanding. Skills, of whatever type, are best learned in context, where the learner is engaged and the application of skills is seen to matter. So, for instance, children learn the skills of construction as a result of their models falling over and revising their strategies; and decide whether to act kindly, or obey the rules, depending partly on what is expected, partly on the consequences, both practical and emotional, of doing so, or not.

The term feedback originates in biology and describes a process which enables an organism to respond to changing circumstances. Adult feedback provides an important source of motivation and reinforcement, encouraging, or otherwise, particular responses, helping children to know whether their actions are appropriate. While we tend to associate feedback with spoken language, it takes many forms – a smile or a sign of approval, a tick or a treat, a wagging finger or worried look. But some types of feedback, from some people, do more to develop intrinsic motivation than others. Quality matters more than quantity.

The most obvious form of positive feedback is verbal praise, though one should not underestimate the effect of a nod or a gesture of reassurance. Such feedback provides recognition and reinforcement and makes adult expectations explicit. However, in Alexander's (1995, p. 206) words, 'praise may not be what it seems. For one thing, it becomes devalued if it is used too often and without discrimination; for another the use of overt praise may be at variance with other messages about children's work which a teacher is conveying and which children readily pick up.' The former can be problematic with very young children, since adults tend to want to praise and never to criticize. And the most important messages are often conveyed less through what adults say, than what they do and think, often unconsciously.

Feedback works in both directions. In Hattie's (2009, p. 4) words, 'it is the feedback to the teacher about what students can and cannot do that is more powerful than feedback to the student'. So, teachers – and other adults – must pay careful attention to, and welcome, errors as opportunities for enhancing learning, and encourage children not to be afraid to make mistakes or articulate what they do not know. This requires a secure emotional climate, where:

- children feel safe to challenge each other and adults, in appropriate and thoughtful ways without fear of repercussions; and
- adults can observe, listen and respond and, in particular, be attuned to the emotional state of individuals and the group.

All too often, adults take little notice of children's ideas and questions, joys and worries. Adults must listen, and attend, to these, rather than dismissing them, in the mad dash for short-term results. We return to other sorts of feedback in subsequent chapters.

Neuroimaging indicates that many areas of the brain are activated when analogies are made, suggesting that multiple connections are taking place. Geake (2009, p. 96) writes that 'the essence of intelligent behaviour lies in making insightful metaphors and analogies' going on to say that 'insightful analogy is necessary for success in a wide range of educational endeavours, including pattern recognition, composition of musical variations, producing and appreciating humour, translation between languages, poetry, classroom exercise and much of everyday speech'. Analogy invites and encourages imagination and connection with what one already knows; and is particularly useful in understanding abstract concepts. The more abstract ideas are, the harder they are to understand, emphasizing the benefit of examples, analogies and metaphors.

The social aspect of learning is more obvious in ethics than, say, mathematics, since finding out what is acceptable (or otherwise) within a particular social context depends on learning from those who are more experienced and knowledgeable. This helps explain why analogy and concrete examples drawn from, or at least related to, the child's own experience are powerful tools in children understanding the abstract, puzzling language of ethics; and why the relationship between adult and child is best seen as like an apprenticeship.

Repetition helps to build neural networks, leading to automatic, non-conscious responses. Habituation helps to develop something akin to 'muscle memory' where one acts in particular ways as if by second nature, without conscious thought. So, for example, I will (usually) hold a door open for someone struggling with a heavy bag or join a queue without barging in, with only limited conscious thought. Claxton (1997) distinguishes between what he calls deliberative and intuitive thinking, which bypasses conscious thought but still has to be learned. Conscious mechanisms work more slowly and deliberately than emotional ones, so that appropriate action, in the moment, relies largely on intuition, learned by regular practice, reinforced by affirmative feedback, so that such actions become automatic.

Rote learning helps to make certain types of behaviour habitual. This might imply that one should drill children into particular patterns of response, but the old saying that practice makes perfect is true only if one is practising in the correct way. Otherwise, one may be reinforcing bad habits. We need, rather, to develop dispositions which Katz and Raths (1985, p. 303) see as 'habits of mind, not mindless habits'. Vygotsky (see Claxton, 2007, p. 118) argued that 'habits of mind' are contagious. So, children's learning behaviours must be reinforced, *in the right way*, and, to use Hattie's (2009) term, be 'over-learned'.

Ethics entails conducting oneself appropriately regardless of whether one will get caught. So, children must learn not to rely primarily on externally imposed norms of behaviour but on setting, and meeting, their own standards of conduct. This requires guidance by those with more experience,

increasingly supported by a more conscious understanding and for internalized reasons. So, 'good habits' in terms of ethics entails more than just
conforming to a set of rules or acting out of fear or deference.

Self-regulation and choice

This section considers the conscious learning mechanisms which tend to
be emphasized in thinking about both learning and morality. These enable a greater ability to regulate emotion, make considered choices and take
personal responsibility. Many feelings, such as shame, guilt and conscience,
associated with morality have a strong cognitive element. But, as discussed
above, emotion and cognition are closely linked and young children's conscious learning mechanisms often do not work efficiently.

Maslow's (1970) hierarchy of needs indicates that higher-order mental
functions depend on more basic needs being met. So, for instance, being
creative, focused and productive depends on:

- having a sense of belonging and feeling accepted/appreciated by others,
  which depends on
- feeling safe, which depends on
- not being dominated by physical needs such as hunger or pain.

While emotion and cognition are closely linked, the former tends to dominate, particularly at times of heightened emotion. Anxiety must be contained if cognitive processes are to operate successfully. Adults can often do
this metacognitively on their own, for example by telling oneself to stop or
slow down as one becomes more agitated; or by walking away from a situation which heightens one's emotional response.

Young children find this harder because they are (usually) less used to
stepping back from the immediate situation; and so act more on impulse.
For instance, a very young child when annoyed or frustrated may lash
out, or cry, or scream. While most older children can act in accordance
with adult expectations most of the time, heightened emotion may make
this harder, or even impossible. I remember one usually well-behaved
8-year-old suddenly refusing to do what he was, quite reasonably, asked.
Although I asked several times quietly and, I thought, unconfrontation-
ally, he increasingly laughed nervously and became withdrawn, until

eventually he was taken out of the room to calm down and returned a few minutes later acting quite normally.

We all have to learn how to respond appropriately when we *feel* angry or jealous, for instance. This does not involve denying or masking such emotions. It is appropriate to be angry at injustice and natural to be jealous. What matters is how we process such feelings and act as a result. Telling children that they do not feel angry or jealous does not help. Nor does saying (whether in words or implicitly) that they should not feel such emotions and should be happy. Rational discussion is, usually, of limited help at the time. Immediate reassurance and support from someone trusted tends to inhibit impulsive responses and enable consideration of how best to act. In the longer-term, learning to regulate conduct rather than simply responding immediately depends on executive function, that is inhibitory control or self-regulation, so that one gains conscious control over feelings and behaviours. The question of how adults can help to develop children's emotional awareness, both of one's own and other people's emotions, is discussed further in Chapter 9.

Executive function helps to enhance working memory – the processes used to store, organize and manipulate information temporarily – and the efficiency with which one uses it. Executive function develops with age, with middle childhood a time when self-regulation becomes easier for most children; and when children are, rightly, expected to act less impulsively and with more consideration of the effect of their actions. This involves metacognition – being aware of, and able to some extent to control, one's own learning processes – but refers to how one regulates emotional as well as cognitive processes.

The discourse on ethics tends to emphasize volition, making conscious choices between what one ought or ought not to do, or at least to choose the better rather than the worse option. An essential aspect of ethics is to take responsibility for one's actions; and of adults' role to enable and encourage children increasingly to do so and support them in doing so. You may, reasonably, think that we should not make excuses for children who behave badly. However, regulating their actions and exercising choice is not easy for many young children and is particularly difficult for a minority, who may need more to be cared for and supported than to be told.

One major challenge is for children (and adults) not just to 'know' how they should act but actually to act accordingly. Think about this incident.

Case study – the gap between knowing and doing

Steve was a 9-year-old from a troubled background who was always getting into difficulties. His answer, when asked why he had done something silly, was usually that he had been told to do so. When I took him outside and told him to lie down in the road, he said that he wouldn't, because that would be stupid and dangerous. I suggested that perhaps he should say that when other children told him to do something silly. But, unsurprisingly, he never really made the connection, at least in changing what he did.

While Steve may have recognized consciously that what he did was silly, this did not stop him acting in that way. This story does not mean that conscious knowledge does not matter. As Nussbaum (2010, p. 81) writes, 'knowledge is no guarantee of good behaviour, but ignorance a virtual guarantee of bad behaviour'. But it illustrates that conscious mechanisms may not be strong enough to alter how people conduct themselves, when under pressure. My lack of success in encouraging Steve to take responsibility for his own actions and not just to copy other children resulted (in part) from my inability to engage him at an appropriate level to think about the possible result of his actions.

While in one sense, we (and children) always have choice, this is constrained by a range of factors such as the law, by taboo, by convention, by culture, by peer group pressure and by power. Those who have influence, resources and power have a greater level of, ability to exercise, choice. In Williams' (2000, p. 102) words, 'a doctrine of the will's power and resourcefulness in constructing and maintaining identities ... cannot but distort and obscure a whole range of facts about people's grossly unequal access to the various commodities on offer for building identities'.

So, many children, even in middle childhood, start, as Steve did, from a position where he found it very hard to exercise real choice. Other, stronger, influences were at work. Like muscles, the ability to make appropriate choices is strengthened with regular practice. However, restricting choice too severely risks children not learning to make considered choices. Learning to regulate one's emotional responses, and not to act on impulse, not only requires time, practice and support, but the chance to have appropriate responses reinforced and inappropriate ones corrected without the fear of rejection or humiliation.

Paradoxically, to develop agency and the ability to make appropriate choices requires structure. Too much choice is overwhelming. For young children, particularly, and those who are least resilient, rules and structures, both explicit and implicit, help to reduce anxiety and to develop and enable the exercise of intentional choice, appropriate to particular situations. While young children must increasingly learn to regulate their responses and conduct and to make conscious choices, doing so involves testing boundaries to learn what types of behaviour are acceptable. This is considered in more detail in Chapter 8.

For adults to emphasize choice and consequence without recognizing how the context of many children's lives tends to overlook how difficult making such choices may be. And some children may easily become discouraged or disengaged when the school's expectations conflict with messages from home and the community. Although this conclusion may be uncomfortable, schools are places where some children, from families where there is a clash of cultures or a history of failure and negative perceptions of schools, find it hard to 'fit in'. Chapter 8 and 10 discuss the implications in more detail.

Williams pleads (2000, p. 51) for the 'protection of the imaginative space of childhood', so that children can learn about choice and consequence, without facing the actual consequences of real choices. Since the ability to think abstractly and executive function develop only gradually and do not work well when anxious, young children often find it hard to make the link between choice and consequence and act accordingly. So, young children, especially those whose prior experience makes self-regulation difficult, benefit from an environment which contains their anxiety and enables them to do so, without having to face the worry of making real choices. Chapter 9 considers how some activities, notably play, drama and stories, lend themselves well to this.

While understanding and exercising choice and consequence is important in children learning to regulate their responses, the parts of the brain most closely associated with making conscious decisions are those which develop latest, with this continuing well into adolescence. The importance of early experience makes it essential for adults to recognize to what extent particular children are able to exercise conscious choice. The ability to do so only develops gradually and will always be harder for some children than others. For some children, in some contexts, this may not be possible. To expect them to do so without a great deal of support may lead to discouragement and disengagement. Predictable and caring relationships help to contain anxiety and so make it easier for such children to maintain their sense of agency.

This chapter has highlighted how a range of learning mechanisms operate in linked ways. The next considers the influence of culture and experience in how children's identity and motivation is created and sustained.

6

Culture, Identity and Motivation

Socialization and identity

While the development of identity is usually associated with adolescence, its roots are established at a very young age. This process is usually seen (e.g. Erikson, 2000; and Harter, 1999) in terms of sequential stages, similar to Kohlberg's model of moral development, described in Chapter 1, with a broadly Piagetian view. To indicate that identity is much more fluid, and its development less linear, we consider briefly the validity of a Piagetian model in general and in the development of beliefs and attitudes.

Donaldson's (1992) research challenged the notion of the hierarchy of progression through consecutive, linear stages. She concluded that, while children only become able developmentally to operate in what she calls a new 'mode', even very young children can operate at a higher level than expected when a task is familiar and makes sense to them, within a context of relationships which engender trust; for instance in understanding a situation from another person's perspective. Subsequently, children, and adults, move between modes, depending on the nature of the task and the context. This suggests that young children learn best within everyday situations and may lead one to question whether development operates in a linear way. A linear view of development seems more plausible in areas such as mathematics or logic than in ethics, where emotions, actions and beliefs matter so much.

Two enduring insights from Piaget are that children must construct their understanding for themselves and cannot do so until they have reached the necessary developmental point. Agency and engagement are vital but, as Vygotsky (1978) showed, learning is reciprocal and social as well as individual, involving incorporation into a culture and the ability to use its tools. How development occurs depends on the interventions of others. As Bruner (1996, p.120) observes, 'the child's mind does not move to higher levels of abstraction like the tide coming in'.

In Pollard's (1985, p. x) words, 'individuals are thought to develop a concept of 'self' as they interpret the responses of other people to their own actions. Although the sense of self is first developed in childhood, . . . it is continually refined in later life and . . . provides the basis for thought and behaviour.' As Wall (2010, p. 41) writes, 'being-in-the-world is not just passively received, actively constructed or forged gradually over a lifetime. Rather, it involves all three at once.' Even when we appear to make conscious choices, such choices are always constrained as a result of our beliefs and prior experience.

Primary socialization, to use Berger and Luckmann's (1967) term, occurs during early childhood, especially within the family. This is when a child learns the attitudes, values and actions appropriate to individuals as members of a particular culture. Subsequently, broader social interaction leads to secondary socialization, but 'the world internalized in primary socialization is . . . much more firmly entrenched in consciousness than worlds internalized in secondary socializations' (1967, p. 154). Early experience imprints itself very deep, as we saw in relation to attachment. For instance, even as a middle-aged man, when with my mother, I tend to respond differently, more anxiously, sometimes defensively, than I would otherwise in similar situations, despite conscious attempts to do otherwise.

Discussing primary socialization, Berger and Luckmann (1967, p. 151) emphasize how 'the significant others who mediate (the) world to (the child) modify it in the course of mediating it' and 'the child takes on the significant others' roles and attitudes, that is internalizes and makes them his own. And by this identification with significant others the child becomes capable of identifying himself, of acquiring a subjectively coherent and plausible identity' (pp. 151–2). So, identity is both individually and socially constructed; that is, we make choices about who we are and who we want to be, but our identity is shaped and constrained by social forces and influences.

While culture and socialization help to shape how we approach, and respond to, new experience, identity or sense of self is not given or static, but created and fluid. As Russell (2007, p. 54) indicates, 'our concept of selfhood is derived from a narrative which links us to those around us from birth'. Since we each belong to many different groups and cultures, our relationship with which constantly changes, identity is a narrative created, and changing, over time. In Taylor's (1989, p. 47) words, 'in order to have a sense of who we are, we have to have a notion of how we have become and of where we are going'.

Identity is retrospective and prospective, describing both who one is and who one may become. It is the story which we tell (in words and other ways) both to ourselves and to others of who we are – and may become. In Macintyre's (1999, p. 221) words:

> the story of my life is always embedded in the story of those communities from which I derive my identity. I am born with a past; and to try to cut myself off from that past, in the individualistic mode, is to deform my present relationships. The possession of an historical identity and the possession of a social identity coincide.

We are not just individuals, but essentially interdependent.

So, identity is closely associated with a sense of belonging and the traditions, the communities, the groups to which we belong help to define us. Group membership is often indicated by markers of identity: either visible, like a cross or a headscarf or a school uniform, or invisible, such as supporting the 'right' team or wearing the latest fashion. Such markers often indicate a sense of belonging and of pride, for instance when associated with a religious tradition or an organization such as a sports team or youth group. Some of these identities are relatively superficial or transient, others more fundamental, with factors such as religion, home language, gender and ethnicity, particularly important sources of identity.

We all belong to many different groups. As a result, each person has, simultaneously, multiple identities or facets of identity; where a boy may be seen, and see himself, as a Hindu, British, a good footballer, a naughty boy; and a girl as someone living in Korea, a little sister, the leader of a group of friends, someone kind to those in trouble. This can easily lead to conflicting loyalties and be a source of confusion to young children, when the demands pull in different directions.

Identity easily comes to depend on superficial and fragile aspects such as appearance and brand. The pressure to belong by wearing the 'right' clothes or liking the latest fashion in music is often very strong. Such external markers of identity have come to matter increasingly for younger children. Not having the newest trainers or mobile phone may seem trivial; but can be the cause of misery or bullying for some children. No wonder that for many children, especially those who are most troubled, the search for identity is so difficult.

Haidt (2012, pp. 84–6) argues that reputation is a much more powerful motivator than principle. Haun and Tomasello (2011) emphasize the strength of human desire to conform and gain social approval and the effect of peer approval even in preschool children. Relationships with, and the response of, trusted adults, and public praise, are major sources of motivation for very young children. So, pointing out those who are sitting up straight or listening carefully to others will usually encourage others to do likewise.

As discussed in Chapter 3, the media and peer pressure present powerful and appealing messages about how one should act if one is to belong. Harter (1999) underlines the essential role of the peer group in the development of children's self-image. She emphasizes that in middle childhood, approaching adolescence, peers become one of the most important sources of children's self-worth. Gaining the approval of adults, especially those who care for them and whom they respect, remains important, but public recognition may lead to embarrassment. The pressure to conform changes somewhat towards fitting in with wider cultural norms with, paradoxically, the search for individual identity often leading towards conformity.

In Chapter 7, we consider further how identity is created, but before that discuss how children learn to understand, and empathize with, other people.

Understanding and responding to other people

As Fox (2005, p. 106) indicates, 'knowing that someone else has different beliefs and different desires to yours is fundamental to understanding their actions'. Very young children tend to be focused on themselves and their own needs. They only gradually become able to understand and take account of other people's feelings, actions and reactions. Doing so is an essential element of developing an ethical viewpoint, which involves recognizing, and reflecting on, the impact of one's (and other people's) actions on other people; and to try to empathize with, and understand, them.

By about 6 months old, infants can tell if they are being looked at and by about 12 months follow and pay attention to what an adult is looking at. Between 18 months and 2 years, children usually start, in their play, to distinguish between reality and pretence. This is the basis of what is called theory of mind, the capacity to attribute wishes, feelings and beliefs to other people to explain their behaviour; and what Donaldson (1992, p. 256) calls decentring – 'avoiding being bound to a single point of view'.

Bloom (2013, p. 31) argues that babies have an innate moral sense – the capacity to make judgements between kindness and cruelty – but rightly points out that morality involves more than this, such as feelings (like compassion) and motivations. While very young children, including babies, can at times show a remarkable level of compassion, they can also be hurtful.

How, and at what age, children understand their own and other people's emotions is very complex. Gradually, young children come to understand that other people have beliefs and desires which vary from their own, and so can make inferences about other people's behaviour and motivation. Thompson (2009, pp. 163–4) indicates that, by the end of the first year, infants demonstrate an awareness of other people's attention, behaving and feeling. In the second year, they start to develop self-referential emotions such as pride, guilt, shame and embarrassment. By the age of 3, they recognize the importance of other people's beliefs and by 5 or 6 begin to perceive people in terms of their individual traits and motives.

Harris (1989, pp. 90–1) argues that 4- and 5-year-olds know about both personal responsibility and standards of acceptability but do not see the relevance of these to their own feelings, whereas by 7 or 8 children do, and so develop an understanding of emotions such as pride and guilt. Harris (1989, p. 94) highlights that experiencing such emotions precedes understanding them, which depends on recognizing the impact on other people, before understanding these emotions more abstractly. So, at about 6 or 7, children can attribute such emotions to their parents and by 8 give examples of themselves feeling such emotions without reference to someone else.

Broadly, this fits with the research cited in Chapter 5 about feelings with a cognitive element only developing in more complex ways in middle childhood. Moreover, it seems likely that recognizing, and understanding, one's own and other people's emotional state develops gradually and une-venly, in real contexts rather than the laboratory. Emotional cues are often misread well into middle childhood, especially by children from cultures and families where emotion is expressed and understood differently. A lack of secure and predictable relationships makes it harder to interpret some-one else's feelings and responses. This helps to explain why many children have more difficulty in interpreting other people's feelings and behaviours. In addition, children on the autistic spectrum find it hard to see the situation from someone else's perspective; and boys are often less capable than girls of regulating their own, or interpreting other people's, emotions.

Empathy is a vaccine against, and antidote to, egocentricity. As Nussbaum (2010, p. 37) suggests, while empathy is not the same as morality, it helps supply some of its crucial ingredients. She (2010, p. 23) writes, 'it is easier to treat people as objects to be manipulated if you have never learned any other way to see them'. So, to understand the consequences of our actions, we must develop, and use, the ability to feel what it might be like to be in the shoes of someone different from oneself.

Baron-Cohen (2011, p. 11) identifies two aspects of empathy, recognition and response, writing that 'empathy is our ability to identify what some-one else is thinking or feeling, and to respond to their thoughts and feeling with an appropriate emotion'. Rather than just recognizing or sympathizing with how someone else is feeling, empathy involves trying to see and under-stand the situation from someone else's perspective in so far as one can; and respond accordingly. Coles (1997) uses the term the 'moral imagination' to describe children learning how others perceive and understand the world, how someone else will feel or react. While such imagination, on its own, is not enough and must be translated into action, it is hard to see how children can learn to act and interact appropriately without imagining how other people feel.

One cannot achieve complete empathy, but can strive towards it. Doing so requires:

- attunement to other people's beliefs and emotional state, but without assuming that they will respond as you do, to avoid projecting one's own feelings on to others;
- practice and imagination, to interpret cues, especially about feelings, and to try and understand situations from perspectives other than one's own.

This is hard when one has limited experience of recognizing one's own and other people's emotional responses; and when intense emotion encourages a focus on oneself. So, for children to develop attributes such as empathy and compassion requires practice and, at times, explicit messages and examples, and reflection on these, to indicate what these entail. While cognitive processes may help children to understand what such terms mean, practical application is necessary to embed these attributes and to counter social pressures not to exercise them.

Chapter 1 discussed the importance of care, and how this is the foundation of morality. Young children need to be loved and cared for, in many different ways. What may be less obvious is the importance of caring for other people, other sentient beings, the world around and how this helps to develop empathy. Caring for others is based on emotion, rather than rationality (see Noddings, 2013, p. 61). Caring-for involves a recognition of, and response to, how others feel or might feel. This is one reason why young children benefit not only from caring for each other but also caring for dolls, or for pets, even where how 'the other' responds is a matter of imagination.

Recognizing that care is mainly seen as a feminine quality, Noddings denies that caring-for is the preserve of girls and women. Such a view, rightly, rejects an essentialist view of men and women (that this is just 'how they are'); and recognizes that anyone's ability to care-for (as opposed to just care-about) depends, in part, on upbringing, practice and context. In particular, boys are often expected, and so learn, to suppress their feelings, as I was, and girls to express them. Even where parents try to avoid this, these patterns are often encouraged by the peer group and wider cultural expectations. Regulating one's emotions and developing intimate relationships is often harder for boys and those with little or no experience of secure relationships. As a result, such children are likely to need more encouragement to express and process their feelings, though not necessarily publicly or always being positive about how they feel. While all people, regardless of gender or background, must try to develop empathy, this will be harder for some than others.

Hargreaves (2003, p. 48) writes that 'caring begins with people you know, people you can see. Sympathy starts with people around us'. While this is so, especially for children, experiencing and understanding both similarities and differences between themselves and other people matters increasingly in a fragmented and diverse world, where one is likely to meet those with different backgrounds, experiences and beliefs.

Nussbaum (2010, pp. 33–4) suggests that being afraid of 'the other', what is alien or threatening to us, is part of our basic instincts and that all human societies have created 'out-groups' who are stigmatized as shameful or disgusting or both. Rowley et al. (2007) conclude that stereotypes have become more embedded by the age of 9 or 10. So, trying to promote thoughtful attitudes towards those who are different and to challenge stereotypes is particularly important by this age. The interlinked nature of emotion and cognition means that this requires not only factual information but a range of experiences to help children understand the world from perspectives other than their own.

It is worth noting the danger of too 'soft' a notion of caring and that caring involves structure, challenge and prohibition at times, a point considered in Chapter 8. But the rest of this chapter returns to what motivates young children.

Rewards and sanctions

Chapter 2 discussed the mixed reasons and motivations for one's actions, indicating that the factors which motivate individuals vary enormously, so that it is hazardous to generalize. Children, like everyone else, are motivated by different factors, depending on the specific situation. What motivates some children may have little effect on others. But we should not assume that what motivates adults will motivate children.

Fear and shame – and in particular having one's misdemeanours made public – are traditionally associated with ensuring good behaviour and discipline. Until recently in most cultures, and still within many, punishment – and the fear of punishment – has been the most common way of imposing discipline and policing morality. For example, many religions give the message that good actions will be rewarded after death and acting in the wrong way lead to eternal punishment. Corporal punishment was common when I was a boy, fifty years ago, and is still used in many societies. The idea of 'being ashamed of yourself' is less commonly used in England than, say, fifty years ago, though still heard for public figures whose reprehensible conduct has been exposed, where they are 'named and shamed'.

Fear is a basic motivator, whether of being hurt, punished or humiliated. But fear does not encourage good conduct for its own sake. Anxiety – the fear of fear – interferes with conscious processes. As we saw in Chapter 5, Maslow's work indicates that higher cognitive processes are impossible when more basic, primal needs dominate.

Shame is more complicated. In Confucianism, a sense of shame is regarded positively, as it encourages one to reflect on how to improve one's behaviour, as with the idea of repentance in Christianity. Shame is closely linked to conscience, and whether one is living up to one's own standards, and one reason why people do not commit misdemeanours. A sense of conscience, which may appear as remorse after the event or pre-emptively to encourage appropriate action, may make it less likely that someone repeats inappropriate actions.

To motivate someone to conduct themselves well, shame must be associated with conscience and an internal motivation to change. A more complex and conscious feeling, which young children only gradually develop, this is not likely to appear at anything other than a simple level until middle childhood; or even later. Indeed, many adults seem to have only a fairly superficial level of conscience. But one must distinguish between a sense of shame – or conscience – about how one has acted, which can be positive, and a sense of shame about who one is, which is destructive.

Expecting many young children to change their behaviour on the basis of shame is unrealistic. And shaming a child in public, is more likely to create a sense of low self-worth and resentment than one of conscience. The danger is that embarrassment, and the fear of public humiliation, will undermine the child's sense of moral identity and agency, particularly when such incidents are regularly repeated. Consider the following example.

Case study – public humiliation

One of my most uncomfortable memories as a teacher was seeing a boy publicly humiliated in a whole-school assembly. He was constantly in trouble and frequently responded aggressively to other children and to staff. Maybe the adult wished to appeal to a sense of shame, though I suspect the actions resulted more from exasperation. But shouting at the child did nothing to make him change his behaviour, but undermined even further his self-esteem and sense of agency; and set a poor example to the other adults and children present.

While adults have a role in correcting anti-social behaviour, one must avoid linking such behaviour to the child's sense of self, particularly in public. Children – we all – at times, do bad or foolish things, but doing so does not mean that one is a bad or foolish person.

Sanctions, such as fear and punishment, do not tend to encourage good behaviour for its own sake. Emphasizing and reinforcing the positive is much more likely to do so. But again one needs to be careful how one does so. While it may be (relatively) easy to persuade children to behave in particular ways through reward and punishment, neither bribery nor fear is a sound basis for moral development. Since ethics entails learning to conduct oneself appropriately (increasingly) because of intrinsic motivation, it is vital *how* children learn to regulate their actions and to conduct themselves, not just *that* they do. As West-Burnham and Huws-Jones, (2007, p. 38) suggest, 'morality that is based on obedience, compliance and the threat of sanction will always be fragile because it is based on external, negative compulsion'.

For very young children, feeling happy and having fun is a major source of motivation. However, in Chapter 2, I argued that ethics involves being motivated by a deeper and longer term sense of one's own and other people's well-being. The question is *how* to encourage young children to strive for, and achieve, this, without being seen as a killjoy.

In recent years, as discussed in Chapters 3 and 4, the use of external incentives has become more common, both in schools and more widely. Performativity is predicated on the ideas that:

- competition and targets act as key motivators, for schools, teachers and individual children;
- goals and targets make visible what is expected; and
- positive feedback and consistent reinforcement of the desired responses will embed these.

This behaviourist approach is often linked to a focus on choice and consequence which tends to presuppose that children can consciously regulate their own behaviour.

Chapter 4 highlighted the current emphasis in schools on behaviour management, often associated with tangible rewards such as stickers and smiley faces for younger children or treats for older ones; and with sanctions, such as a reprimand or loss of privileges, which help to make explicit the boundaries of what is acceptable. More generally, material reward and competition are widely regarded as powerful motivators to work hard and behave well.

Tangible rewards are often effective in the short term in managing behaviour, and reinforcing conduct deemed appropriate, especially with very young children and those who find self-regulation difficult. Most children 'know' how to conduct themselves even when they do not necessarily do so, and there is a small minority who don't seem to know and may rely heavily on explicit messages backed by external rewards. However, extrinsic motivators usually become ineffective in the longer term and do not help build up, indeed may undermine, intrinsic motivation, which is the key to self-discipline. Rewards, such as stickers, work only up to a point, and sanctions can easily become ineffective. Those who are punished regularly seem to respond least to punishment, whereas those who are most afraid of it may need the threat of it least. So, rewards and sanctions must be used carefully and be temporary, like scaffolding, rather than props, if they are not to create dependence on extrinsic motivators.

The current educational culture emphasizes competition, with children encouraged to 'aim higher'. In some respects, this is helpful. Competition can be a great motivator, as it has been for me. This has a basis in the chemistry of the brain. A certain level of stress hones one's readiness and ability to perform. So, performing well in music or sport, in exams or in a quiz, is often enhanced by competition against others, but this may not lead to caring or sympathetic attitudes. Competitive sport, for instance, *can* help children to learn to win and to lose gracefully; but it may develop highly individualized, even ruthless, dispositions.

Pressure may motivate some children, but demotivate others, especially those with a low sense of agency and self-esteem. Competition between those who start at much the same point may motivate both, but when between those with very unequal abilities often leads to the weaker person giving up and the stronger one being insufficiently challenged. So, competition with other people does not work well where there is a wide discrepancy of abilities and is a poor basis for developing caring relationships and attitudes.

Competition can also involve trying to improve on one's own 'previous best'. Such an approach can be a powerful motivator to act well, especially when linked to personal, achievable goals and targets. For most adults and children, knowing what to aim for, and what to do to achieve this, is helpful. However, Noddings (2013, p. 146) argues that 'for students to engage a subject matter directly they must be free of the mediation of precise objectives'. This seems to be so particularly in areas, such as ethics, where imagination is necessary and where answers are provisional and uncertain. Developing such areas requires space for exploration, rather than a narrowly defined route map.

A sense of power – or powerlessness – is a much stronger influence on motivation than those who are motivated or successful recognize. Such people often do not recognize what motivates those who are less so. An over-emphasis on performance may exclude some children, possibly unwittingly. For instance, those who do not feel that they have much chance of success or that their interests and talents are taken notice of are less likely to try. A lack of respect for what children value tends to lead to disengagement. For example, if a child is very expert in computer games or has a deep knowledge of his religious heritage, but these skills and this knowledge are not valued in school, the child soon recognizes this.

Even more profoundly, the structure of schooling is not neutral in terms of motivation. In Brantlinger's (2003, p. 13) words, 'because (working class and lower income families) rarely benefit from it, the competitive school structure does not play the same motivating role for them as for middle class students. Class advantage may be invisible to those who benefit, but subordinates are acutely aware of barriers to opportunity.' This helps to explain why creating an inclusive environment, where all children's background and beliefs are valued, is so important, yet difficult. The 'moral order' of schools, discussed in Chapter 8, involves being genuinely inclusive of those who are easily excluded, by protecting them from, and equipping them to deal with, barriers to inclusion. This entails taking account of, and valuing, the 'funds of knowledge' which children bring but are often ignored or devalued in formal settings.

Rewards and sanctions may help in motivating children in the short term and are at times necessary to make explicit the boundaries of what is acceptable; but have significant limitations in developing intrinsic motivation. The next section considers factors more likely to do so.

Mindsets, goals and relationships

Dweck's work on motivation and personality development emphasizes that 'people's beliefs about themselves . . . can create different psychological worlds, leading them to think feel and act differently in identical situations' (2000, p. xi). This helps to explain why children's responses to the same situation vary and it is sometimes difficult to understand why they – we all – act in any particular way.

Identity is closely linked to self-esteem and (perceived) status. As Deakin Crick and Goldspink (2014, p. 30) observe, identity is profoundly shaped by the stories that other people tell about a person. Self-concept affects how children remain engaged and motivated. If a child perceives herself as stupid or inadequate, or as successful or resourceful, she is more likely to become so. She has to believe that she can change and to imagine, and so help to create, what she might become. If beliefs and motivation are not to be brittle, children must internalize from an early age a robust sense of identity of how they should act and interact; and to do so they benefit from guidance and encouragement more than preaching and haranguing.

Dweck emphasizes that children must have a sense of agency and what she calls 'mastery-oriented qualities' – broadly, those which enable one to cope with setbacks – and a 'growth mindset': a belief that change is possible and that ability is not inherent and fixed, but can be enhanced by effort and support.

Dweck challenges the belief that mastery-oriented qualities:

- are more likely to be displayed by children with high levels of attainment;
- are directly fostered by success in school; or
- depend on children's confidence in their intelligence.

While a low level of self-esteem leads easily to disengagement, high self-esteem does not necessarily lead to a secure sense of self as a learner. Self-confidence which is not robust in the face of challenge and setbacks is worthless; and may be damaging. Dweck argues that, without a growth mindset, high levels of performance often make children concerned about failure. While we tend to assume that success leads to greater success, Dweck (2000, p. 1) writes that 'success in itself does little to boost (students') desire for challenge or their ability to cope with setbacks . . . (and) can have quite the opposite effect', especially when it makes them afraid of failure – and so of risk-taking.

Donaldson (1992, p. 7) argues that setting goals for ourselves, often very diverse ones, is central to how we learn. In the short term, externally set goals motivate many children, but these easily lead to children focusing only on what is being taught or tested and avoiding lateral or divergent thinking. Goals and targets are motivating only when realistic and are more so when set by the person to whom they apply.

Motivation is greater when one sees the point of an activity. A sense of purpose – understanding why rather than just complying – and the desire for attention and approval, in a context of relationships of trust, tend to be stronger long-term motivators, especially for young children, than extrinsic factors such as rewards, sanctions and targets. Engagement stems from a belief that an activity matters and that one can do something about it – a feeling of mastery, autonomy and adequacy, which young children often lack in formal settings where they do not feel in control. No amount of adult scaffolding can ever make up for a child's disengagement. The least experienced or confident learners need the most sensitive support if they are to remain engaged and motivated.

Dweck distinguishes between what she calls performance and learning goals. She (2000, pp. 151–2) writes that both sorts of goal are 'entirely natural, desirable and necessary . . . The problem with performance goals arises when proving ability becomes so important to students that it drives out learning goals.' To create a growth mindset, praise should be positive but not unthinkingly so and linked to specific actions and attributes, to reinforce these.

Dweck makes a convincing case for praising children for the attributes of successful learners rather than for intelligence or completing easy tasks, writing that, far from instilling confidence, praise (for smartness) can lead students 'to fear failure, avoid risks, doubt themselves when they fail, and cope poorly with setbacks' (2000, p. 2). And, as summarized in Claxton (2005, p. 17), 'self-esteem is much more potent when it is "won through striving whole-heartedly for worthwhile ends, rather than derived from praise, especially praise that may be only loosely related to actual achievement"'. So, while young children need praise and reinforcement, constant praise, regardless of children's effort, can easily lead to them not recognizing the importance of hard work, persistence and trying again.

While rewards and grades may be intended to provide positive feedback, Dweck (2000) argues that reliance on these tends to enhance ego- rather than task-related involvement. In other words, they focus attention on aspects such as ability rather than what one has done. Such an emphasis undermines self-esteem for those who are unsuccessful and makes it fragile for high-attainers. So, feedback should focus on learning qualities and behaviours, such as persistence and thoughtfulness. This helps to create and sustain a growth mindset, the view that the child has agency and is capable of change, not a victim of what is unalterable.

Young children's engagement and creativity result from whether they see a task as worthwhile and the context and relationships make them feel safe enough to take risks. Chapter 5 emphasized young children's search for predictability and meaning; and the role of relationships in helping to achieve this. Predictability, consistency and care matter particularly for those who are young, unused to secure and trusting relationships or in unfamiliar situations. Very young children are strongly motivated to please adults who care for them; and are more 'biddable', or easily influenced, in terms of behaviour than older children. Children in middle childhood must, and do, become less dependent on such relationships and learn to cope with unpredictability and uncertainty, to make conscious, responsible choices. But they continue to require support in this, given the strength and influence of pressures from the peer group and wider culture.

While relationships between children and adults matter, one must be careful to ensure that these are appropriate. Children must feel secure if conscious mechanisms are to work well, but not so protected that their sense of agency is diminished. Consistency does not entail adults responding like automatons regardless of context, since the reciprocal nature of learning means that adults must be attuned, and try to respond, to individual children's circumstances and comments. And as Nussbaum (2010, p. 6) argues, one defining feature of ethical behaviour is that 'relationships (are) not of mere use and manipulation'. Adult–child relationships are asymmetrical, in terms of power and control. Chapter 8 considers the implications of this paragraph further, but for now let us remember that adults can easily misuse their power, even when their intentions are benign.

This discussion raises the dilemma of how prescriptive should adults be. For those who are too definite, the danger is that young children become dependent on rules and extrinsic motivation and older ones unable to exercise discernment about the context. For those who rely too much on implicit messages, many young children, especially the least resilient, may be left uncertain about how to act. Too rigid a structure is likely to constrict some children, too loose a one to confuse others. But the structures, like scaffolding, must be temporary if children are not to become dependent on these.

Learning does not just involve an intricate configuration of internal learning mechanisms but an even more complex web of processes, with external factors such as culture, relationships, example and expectations helping to create a sense of identity. Praise, affirmation and attention tend to be more powerful motivators than put-downs, punishment and competition, with the value ascribed to children's culture, background and 'funds of knowledge' – what they bring from outside school – having a strong influence. Chapter 7 considers the implications for the development of character and moral identity; and subsequent chapters how adults can help to shape children's identity by their expectations, feedback and responses.

7

Learning to Live a Good Life

Character, virtues and values

This section explores three terms associated with ethics – character, virtue and values – and consider some benefits and disadvantages of using these, recalling how problematic language can be.

The Shorter Oxford English Dictionary's definition of moral starts '*of or pertaining to human character and behaviour as good or bad.*' Yet the term character is not much used in relation to education, in the United Kingdom, though more so in the United States and many Asian cultures. At least partly, this seems to result from it being associated, in England, with a view captured in phrases such as 'backbone' and 'stiff-upper-lip' – related to doing one's duty doggedly, regardless of the consequences, traditionally associated with elite schools. So, character has connotations, in England, of male, upper-class attitudes and behaviour, with its formation related to physical discomfort and denial of emotion. Despite this, it remains a useful idea to describe deeply embedded aspects of one's identity.

Chapter 2 indicated that virtue ethics involves developing a range of attributes or traits which reflect, and shape, the sort of person one is, and aspires to be. These are what constitute one's character. Dewey (2002, p. 38) describes character as the 'interpenetration of habits', indicating that it consists of a complex mixture of deep-rooted elements, mostly formed without conscious effort, like identity. Sennett (1998, p. 10) argues that 'character particularly focuses upon the long-term aspect of our emotional experience. Character is expressed by loyalty and mutual commitment, or through the pursuit of long-term goals, or by the practice of delayed gratification for a future end.' Essentially, character is about how one acts and interacts when not overseen or observed, or influenced directly by the promise of reward or fear of punishment. So, character describes an amalgam of embedded attributes which inform and encourage intrinsic motivation, or otherwise.

While not unchanging, character remains fairly constant and influences, rather than determines, how one acts; and can, of course, be bad as well as good, or more often mixed. Character provides a framework which influences action, but responses are strongly affected by the immediate environment. Apparently responsible people may, at a football match or in a crowd, act out of character. We tend to lose self-control, and act uncharacteristically, when others around us act in ways which appeal to aspects of ourselves we have otherwise learned to control. This is true for everyone, but particularly so for young children, because silly behaviour is often attractive and their mechanisms to regulate emotional responses are (usually) less well developed. Think how easily one or two children 'acting-out' can lead otherwise well-behaved ones to copy them. The influence of the environment helps to explain why good people sometimes do bad things and bad people good things, but good people act thoughtfully and selflessly more frequently.

As indicated in Chapter 1, the term character education is used in different ways. However, Arthur (2003, pp. 28–9) observes that 'character education is not identical with moral education since character development involves the emergence of certain enduring traits, only some of which can be classed as moral'. For instance, a strong character implies resilience and determination not to give up in the face of difficulty. Character is broader in scope than morality. Since the boundary between the moral and non-moral is blurred, the idea of character is helpful in not detaching those attributes associated with morality from others to be encouraged and cultivated.

We shall return to what these attributes are. However, attributes are different from, though linked to, behaviours. So, for instance, perseverance is a behaviour which is a manifestation of, and helps to build, resilience; and acting empathetically is an indication of thoughtfulness, and helps to embed it. Making these behaviours habitual helps to strengthen such attributes.

While, in many respects, moral development involves internalizing messages without reliance on conscious processes, a major challenge is how to help young children to make abstract concepts more 'visible', to use Hattie's (2009) term. Identifying, exemplifying and discussing what abstract qualities look like in practice helps children to understand what they entail and how to embed them. Children and adults need a vocabulary of ethics to identify specific actions and attributes to be encouraged, or discouraged. The term character is too broad, but virtues and values provide a more accessible basis for such a language.

The word virtue has a similar problem to that of character since it may be seen as rather old-fashioned, for instance being used of women who have remained sexually faithful; or implying 'too good to be true'. And its opposite – vice – has fallen out of use not least because of being associated with unalterable wickedness. However, virtue is closely associated with character, since virtuous persons are those of good character – and vice versa. Virtues tend to be, but are not exclusively, associated with ethics, so that for instance we talk of patience or tidiness as virtues.

Virtue involves emotional as well as cognitive responses, since in Macintyre's (1999, p. 149) words, 'virtues are dispositions not only to act in particular ways but to feel in particular ways'. And, as Winston (1998, p. 65) writes, 'with emotional knowledge can come moral knowledge for to learn the virtues is to learn particular feelings and particular emotional responses'.

As indicated in Chapter 2, virtue is mainly developed by practice and consists of finding the best course of action between two extremes (or vices) – what I called the Goldilocks approach. How virtues should be applied in practice is determined by the specific context. Finding the appropriate course of action requires discernment about the particular context and the people within it.

Virtue should be seen in social rather than individual terms. As Winston (1998, p. 174) argues, 'virtues exist and are defined by the communities which practice them'. This may be seen as an advantage of an approach based on virtue, since in a complex, changing society, we all live within a range of communities which may privilege different virtues; or as a weakness, if one is worried about relativism. However, the situated nature of virtue is a strength when working with young children as this helps to relate abstract ideas to real situations and recognizes the importance of feeling.

The term values is attractive and widely used, partly to fill the perceived void left by the absence of religion as the basis for ethics. In education, business and sport, shared values are frequently emphasized, as the basis of teamwork and a sense of collective purpose. The language of values recognizes that ethics is about feelings and relationships, not just rationality. In Winston's (1998, p. 6) words, 'to talk of values is to talk the language of feeling as well as reason, of commitment and conviction as well as duty and obligation'.

Halstead (1996, p. 5) defines values as 'principles, fundamental convictions, ideals, standards or life stances which act as general guides to behaviour or as points of reference in decision-making or the evaluation of beliefs or action and which are closely connected to personal integrity and personal identity'. While this definition is helpful, three problems arise with the term values.

The first is that the language of values tend to be vague rather than specific. In some respects this can be a strength, providing a rule of thumb about how to act. However, the term values is used to describe both:

- what actually happens, and
- what one wishes to happen

that is both descriptively and aspirationally. Ideally, these coincide and values-as-articulated fit with values-as-lived. In more academic language, espoused theories – beliefs, attitudes and values that people express – and theories-in-use should be congruent (see Argyris and Schon, 1974). But this is rarely so in practice and the language of values easily blurs the distinction.

The second is that values refers sometimes to the qualities that an individual does, or should, manifest; and sometimes to the beliefs of a group or a society. Young children, especially, need to know the attributes which they should aspire to live by and for these to be as specific and related to their own lives as possible. The language of values is often used too generally, without emphasizing that what these entail for the individual must always depend on judgement about the context; and that as we shall see in the next section what values mean in practice is rarely simple.

The third difficulty is that 'values' is often used to try to create a false consensus, for instance when politicians appeal to shared values, even when different sections of society or cultures have differing beliefs or ways of understanding the same word. This is particularly so with an appeal to universal values, such as respect or fairness, words which may be understood very differently. Since this point requires more detailed discussion, we return to it in the next section.

So, the terms virtues and values help to identify desirable, but abstract, attributes and traits of character and can provide a good basis for a vocabulary of ethics. They have the advantage, for many people, of not being associated closely with religion; but disadvantages as outlined above. The practical implications of this discussion for how they are best used should become clearer as we consider specific values and virtues.

Are values and virtues universal?

In this section, I address the question of whether – and to what extent – values and virtues are universal or specific to particular cultures, recalling the debate, mentioned in Chapter 2, between universalism and particularism. For now, I make no distinction between values and virtues, but at the end of the next section indicate my preference for how these terms may be used with children.

Many people have an intuitive resonance with the idea that we all have common needs and share common values. Indeed, a group (usually of fairly like-minded people) will often arrive at a broadly agreed list.

Let us look at three lists. The first in Table 7.1 is the Olympic and Paralympic values, the second, in Table 7.2, the twenty-two values used in Values-based Education, discussed in more detail in Chapter 10.

Table 7.1 The Olympic and Paralympic Values

Respect	Excellence	Friendship	
Determination	Inspiration	Equality	Courage

Table 7.2 The values recommended for Values-based Education

Appreciation	Caring	Cooperation	Courage	Hope
Freedom	Patience	Understanding	Honesty	Love
Respect	Trust	Simplicity	Humility	Peace
Friendship	Tolerance	Responsibility	Quality	Unity
	Happiness	Thoughtfulness		

Source: Eaude, 2004, p. 5.

Table 7.3 The nine values adopted in Values Education in Australia

Care and compassion	Doing your best	'Fair go'
Freedom	Honesty and trustworthiness	Integrity
Respect	Responsibility	Understanding, tolerance and inclusion

Source: National Framework for Values Education in Australian Schools, 2005.

Table 7.3 gives a shorter list of nine values adapted from this approach and adopted in a large programme in Australian schools, described in Lovat and Toomey (2007).

Some of these, like honesty and respect, are more closely related to ethics than others, such as 'doing your best' or freedom. It is hard to be against any of them, though one might question whether some are really values; or to what extent they provide more than a very general indication how one should act in practice. While such values may seem to be universal, the situation becomes more complex, when one digs below the surface.

First, some values deemed very important in some cultures and religions are not included. Any list has to be selective, but for instance where is justice? Or modesty? Or patriotism?

Second, in Alexander's (1995, pp. 24–5) words, 'values are not absolutes. They are by their nature contestable and contested'. Even within a coherent group, differences of both content and emphasis emerge as soon as one becomes specific. As Katayama (2004, p. 70) writes, 'in a plural society like ours people agree in valuing virtues like justice and honesty but do not share the same interpretation of these terms . . . The more detailed interpretation such words are given, the more difficult it is to achieve a broad consensus.' Katayama goes on to suggest that how values are put into practice would in many cases be agreed by educators. However, this underplays the point that individuals must decide the appropriate course of action in the specific context: a problem when different values, or virtues, point in contrasting directions.

Third, an emphasis on universal values runs the risk of assuming, or creating, a false consensus which takes too little account of the contested nature of morality and of presenting ethics too simply; rather than recognizing that real life often involves uncomfortable choices. To claim that values are universal tends to shy away from conflict and difference, in the search for consensus. Many values may be common to most cultures, but others are more culturally specific; and the greater the diversity of a group or society, the more likely legitimate differences will exist. And even if values were universal, at times different values clash.

Finally, the idea of universal values carries the (usually implicit) assumption which privileges the liberal values of relatively rich and 'developed' countries (see Haydon, 2004); and so fails to recognize that what is valued changes over time and differs between cultures. To illustrate this, let us consider, briefly, five potentially controversial attributes:

- patriotism
- ambition
- humility
- modesty, and
- deference

and then three more closely associated with ethics and likely to be seen as universal:

- fairness
- respect, and
- honesty.

In many countries, notably newly independent ones, patriotism is an attribute, or a virtue, which most adults wish to instil in children, for instance in honouring the flag as in the United States. Even in England where there is greater reticence about expressing patriotism, it has been seen historically as a virtue, notably at times of crisis. Such a view has been undermined to some extent by scepticism about 'my country right or wrong', so that individual choice is now often seen as more appropriate than unthinking obedience. So, while patriotism may be seen as a virtue, what it actually entails is more debatable.

Ambition is encouraged in many societies, especially Anglo-Saxon and many East Asian societies. An absence of ambition may suggest a lack of drive, though many people may be suspicious of an excess of ambition, especially for one's own aggrandizement. In some societies, including many aboriginal cultures, individual success matters less than collective action, while the individual's drive to succeed is encouraged in others, such as the United States. Ambition is closely linked to aspiration, a precondition for successful learning, particularly for those whose family background or culture results in low levels of confidence and self-esteem. So, one may be suspicious of some of its manifestations and whether ambition is a virtue seems to depend on what one is ambitious *for*.

Humility is seen in many religious traditions, such as Christianity, as profoundly important. However, it would have been scorned by the Ancient Greeks, as it is in the macho world of the streets in modern Western countries. While pride is the opposite of humility, pride in one's own and other people's achievements is usually seen as appropriate. The problem arises when pride is manifested to 'show off' or to excess.

Modesty is central to most Islamic and South Asian traditions. A loss of modesty represents a serious stain on character, especially for girls and women. This relates to a more collective, rather than just a personal, responsibility. The importance of *izzat*, family honour, may be hard to understand in a celebrity culture which seems to make a virtue of immodesty, both in terms of sexuality and publicizing oneself.

The reduced level of deference towards authority was highlighted in Chapter 3, with the benefit, and the disadvantage, of encouraging children to be less accepting, automatically, of what adults say. Deference towards one's elders used to be widely regarded as appropriate and still is in many cultures, notably those in East Asia. Yet, contemporary Western culture seems not to value deference towards those with more experience any more than it does humility and modesty.

These examples indicate that what is valued changes across times and cultures. But, surely, some values, such as respect, fairness and honesty are universal? Who could be against respecting other people? Or acting fairly? Or telling the truth? Yet even these are more problematic than one may think. As soon as one delves into what this means in practice, the apparent consensus starts to unravel.

For instance, does fairness mean treating everyone the same or taking account of their particular background or needs? The former overlooks the extent to which some people's prior experience and existing power or knowledge give them more chance of success. And the latter may lead to entrenching, rather than challenging, existing aspirations and beliefs deriving from culture and background. Similarly, does fairness mean equality or proportionality – broadly speaking everyone having the same or what they deserve? Does it imply providing everybody with the same opportunity; or working towards similar outcomes, and so seeking to rectify existing inequalities? Although these may seem rather academic debates, the difficulty becomes clearer when one has to apply the term 'fairness' in practice, such as when two siblings argue about what the older or younger one should be allowed to do; or when a teacher has to choose a few children from a class for an opportunity not available to all.

Respect is one attribute commonly regarded as essential by both children and adults, including me, given my emphasis on relationships and empathy. But should one respect everyone equally, including racists and criminals? Or show more respect to those in positions of power or status? Or to those less capable of looking after themselves? I am caught between a wish to respect those who are wiser, but not to show automatic respect, when it is not reciprocated. Many adolescents are concerned that others should not 'diss' (for disrespect) them; and angry at those who look down on what the adolescents regard as important. So, it is legitimate to ask to what extent one should show respect for those one believes to be wrong or feckless; and those who do not demonstrate respect.

Surely everyone can agree that honesty is a virtue universally to be cultivated? Yes, but only to a point. Should a child be expected to say what she thinks about another child whom she dislikes? Or an adult to be honest to a child who is seriously ill? And if so, how? Honesty must often be tempered by other qualities such as compassion and sensitivity.

This discussion indicates that values and virtues are not universal, however much we may wish it; and that seeing them as such downplays the extent of legitimate diversity of views and conduct. It does not mean that one should not strive towards such ideals, and encourage children to do so; but even very young children need to recognize that what these ideas entail can be complicated and contested. So, whose values and which virtues should moral educators espouse and promote?

Whose values, which virtues for an uncertain future?

This section discusses the attributes and qualities required for an uncertain future, where many of the old certainties, provided by parents and school and, for some, religion may seem inaccessible or inapplicable. In particular, it considers how to decide which values and virtues should be espoused in a world where these are not universally agreed.

One way is to appeal to the values of a group, such as British values, but in trying to identify these one soon encounters difficulties. Would one include tolerance, or freedom, or democracy, for instance? Many from ethnic minority groups would doubt the reality of the commitment to tolerance and that to freedom might be questioned by those no longer allowed to take part in fox-hunting or smoke in public places. And while a better case may be made for democracy, in the sense of holding regular elections, a brief consideration of different societies soon indicates contrasting views of what is meant by democracy. As with universal values, there are different perspectives on what specific words mean in practice; and there is often a mismatch between values-as-described and values-as-lived, between what a society (claims it) aspires to and what actually happens.

Similar problems occur if one tries to define Christian values. Cooling (2010) discusses the list prepared by the Church of England to support Church schools. He (p. 29) writes:

> many . . . would be welcomed by non-church schools, for example thankfulness, endurance and compassion. However, others would probably raise an eyebrow, including creation, wisdom and humility. The big surprise . . . is *koinonia* . . . defined as 'that which is in common and is often translated as fellowship'.

There is not enough space to discuss the detail of what Christian values involve, though a consensus even within Christianity would be unlikely. However, Cooling highlights the problem of a slide 'from assuming that shared values are uncontroversial *because people do in fact share them* to assuming that people ought to share them *because they are obvious common sense*' (p. 29). The foreword makes the important point that 'the virtues which should characterize Christian education . . . are distinctively Christian but they are not necessarily uniquely Christian' (p. 9). So, while it is (at best) difficult to identify particular values or virtues as distinctive of a faith (or other) group, one can identify a loose group of qualities associated with belonging to that group, without excluding those outside the group entirely. Such an approach is necessary in settings like schools if they are to be inclusive of those of all faiths and of none.

It may be argued that in a context based on particular, explicit beliefs and values, such as a Roman Catholic school, after school sessions at the mosque or a sports club, it is reasonable to expect everyone to adopt these. However, this may militate against an inclusive approach, hinder children from developing an enhanced understanding of what these entail and prevent them from learning to deal with the diversity of belief that they will encounter in an increasingly diverse and globalized world. I suggest, in Chapter 8, that, in practice, one should establish collective expectations, applicable to a particular context, but without tying these too closely to any one set of beliefs and presenting them as universal.

Whatever our role, we seem to be in a trap because:

- an appeal to universal values is no longer appropriate in a diverse and globalized world, although some are broadly agreed; and
- the attributes, or virtues, to be encouraged vary between cultures and must be applied depending on the context, and so should be a matter of constant debate and reflection.

In Eaude (2008b), I tried to find a way out of this trap by drawing on Kekes' work, cited in Frowe (2007, pp. 275–8), on primary and secondary values. Kekes describes primary values as those which set the necessary, though not sufficient, conditions for all good lives; and may be seen as (in practice) applicable to all. Primary values are based on a 'thin' view which sets out the minimum required for a good life or a good society. Kekes (see Frowe, 2007, p. 276) sets out three categories of needs, those of:

- the self, for instance physiological and psychological;
- intimacy, for example to establish close personal relationships with some people; and
- social order, such as the establishment of some authority, the existence of institutions and conventional practices.

Secondary values, while dependent on primary ones, change according to culture or individual preference. They 'enrich life by presenting possibilities beyond the requirements set by primary values' (cited in Frowe, 2007, p. 276). The primary values represent necessary conditions for good lives, while secondary values constitute a set of optional beliefs which some, but not all, individuals may adopt. This distinction:

- differentiates between what is essential to human thriving and what reflects the diversity of human aspiration and preference; and
- recognizes the reality that different cultures and societies place varying levels of importance on different qualities and the rights of individuals to pursue their own conceptions of the good life.

Such an approach draws on precedents which emphasize some virtues or values more than others. For example, the Ancient Greeks highlighted prudence, courage, perseverance and generosity and there is a long tradition within Christianity of the 'cardinal virtues' – prudence, justice, temperance and courage. The obvious difficulty is to decide which virtues or values are primary and which are secondary. Paradoxically, this seems to me a strength, because it promotes debate about which matter most in any particular setting, leaving open the opportunity, and encouraging respect, for cultural and individual diversity.

An appeal to universal values is attractive for those working with young children, in providing a simple framework about how children and adults should act and interact and a common vocabulary to discuss this. But such an approach tends to oversimplify, making it hard for children to develop over time the mature and sophisticated discernment necessary in a complex and changing world. For example, most decisions on appropriate conduct depend on choosing between different virtues, such as loyalty and honesty when asked to break a confidence to protect a friend; or finding a balance between conflicting virtues – should I be brave or loyal? – and between extremes, each of which – telling the whole truth or lying – would be inappropriate. For adults to prescribe what to do in any particular context and present simple and definite solutions may inhibit a deeper understanding and underplays the extent to which individuals have to steer a thoughtful course through conflicting demands.

Some of the values and virtues listed above may seem rather complicated and abstract, with very young children. Eaude (2004) indicates that in practice most of those in Table 7.2 were fairly easily understood even by very young children, although some, such as humility and patience, proved more difficult. However, as with any language, understanding grows through use; and it is part of the skill of adults to use and adapt these terms depending on the children's age and experience. The language used with children needs to be accessible but not too simple. While a vocabulary of ethics can be framed as values or virtues, my preference is to use:

- virtues for the attributes to be encouraged in children and adults; and
- values to describe those espoused by an institution.

In exploring the question – whose values, which virtues? – I have suggested that adults face a tension between standing up for, and embodying, what they believe to matter and being too prescriptive about how children should act and interact. Chapter 10 discusses how this can be resolved and suggests that a strength of virtue ethics is flexibility, so that the specific attributes to be encouraged can be adapted for younger and older children, for religious and other settings.

Implications for how young children learn to live a good life

This section summarizes the implications of the last three chapters for moral, and character, education and highlights key issues for adults discussed in more detail in the next three chapters.

Chapter 5 indicated that the learning mechanisms associated with emotion and cognition are linked, though the former operate more quickly. Young children's cognitive processes tend to work inefficiently, particularly at times of intense emotion. Haidt (2012) summarizes extensive research indicating that moral judgements are made intuitively, based on emotional responses, with reasoning and rationalizations usually following. Character education involves training what Haidt calls the emotional elephant, not just the conscious rider.

In Evans' (2001, p. 46) words:

> the moral capacities that most of us have, . . . are based not on a set of rules like the instructions in a computer program, but on emotions like sympathy, guilt and pride. The development of moral capacities in children is, therefore, not likely to be helped by teaching them a set of commandments and precepts, unless their emotional capacities are also well nurtured . . . Without moral sentiments to guide your moral reasoning, you would only ever obey the letter of the law rather than the spirit.

Learning how to respond appropriately to emotion and to be self-disciplined is a complex process, taking time, requiring support and not involving just following a script, or rationalizing. Rather, it requires observing how a range of people regulate their behaviour, practising in different situations and having appropriate actions reinforced. This is not to say that children should not think about how to act and interact. Of course, they should. Encouraging and supporting children to think though possible courses of action and their consequences becomes increasingly important in middle childhood (and beyond) because of the greater influence of social, cultural and peer group pressures. Without secure foundations these conscious processes will be rootless. What must underpin such action and thinking are embedded attributes and dispositions, such as empathy and thoughtfulness, which take account of other people's needs and feelings.

Developing such attributes depends mostly on example and habit. In Oakeshott's words, 'by living with people who habitually behave in a certain way we acquire habits of conduct in the same way we acquire our native language', by being exposed to this every day, by imitation and thus by habit (see Erricker and Erricker, 2000, p. 98). And as Katayama (2004, pp. 70–1) writes, 'children are initiated into the practices of virtues from early childhood. Children learn, or mis-learn, how to be just, honest and temperate from parents and teachers in daily, uncomplicated situations long before they start to reflect on what justice, honesty and temperance are.'

Attributes and dispositions are caught, as if by osmosis, more than (directly) taught, though this process is supported by language, both one's own and other people's. For instance, creativity or teamwork are learned primarily through practice in an environment which encourages these. Experiences such as working together, solving real problems or rehearsing and performing a play, help embed qualities such as cooperation and collaboration. Attributes such as empathy and thoughtfulness – and the disposition to manifest these – are deepened by practice in real-life contexts, rather than just in programmes and lessons designed for this purpose. These issues are discussed in more detail in Chapter 9.

Many approaches to character education, such as Lickona's (1992), are based on separate programmes in schools, relying mainly on cognitive processes. In contrast, my argument is that developing character, and learning to live a good life:

- takes place throughout life and is more a matter of the heart than the head; and
- is a cumulative and gradual, though not a linear, process, involving increasingly deep learning.

Rather than memorization and replication of information, deep learning involves the application and internalization of knowledge, so that it becomes 'intuitive and fundamental to the identity of the person' (West-Burnham and Huws Jones, 2007, p. 48). In particular, character education must nurture and sustain a sense of moral identity, by which I mean a sense of 'what sort of person am I? and what sort of person do I wish to become?' Chapter 6 presented identity as a narrative – the story one constructs and tells of oneself – which is shaped, but not determined, by one's culture and background and influenced by, but not dependent on, other people's perceptions. Such a sense of self is what other people can help to change, to strengthen or undermine, particularly for young children.

As Salmon (1995, p. 63) indicates:

> identity . . . is forged out of interaction with others. Who we are is inextricably bound up with who we are known to be. Children bring to school very particular family identities, identities which facilitate some kinds of learning, but inhibit others. Social relationships with other young people, and participation in school culture, act to produce new dimensions in the sense of self, which frame the meaning of pupils' classroom conduct and closely govern what they may and may not do.

Relationships with adults whom they can trust, and who increasingly trust them, in everyday situations, over time, provide children with predictability and consistency. Such relationships exert a strong influence on young children's self-concept and identity; and have the potential to create secure identities and, at least to some extent, heal damaged ones.

Identity, and with it self-image, is built on a sense of oneself (and how others see one), involving not only the more obvious external markers, such as clothing which identifies one as a boy, a Sikh or a member of team, but of a much subtler amalgam of qualities for instance as a reader or an artist, as friendly and kind or prickly and aggressive. While being born as a girl or a Christian, as physically able or in poverty does not determine identity and self-concept, it affects it; and living with an abusive father or a highly aspirational mother will affect a child's view of himself and his expectations. The formation of identity involves negotiating between different aspects of how we understand ourselves and how others may see us.

Each person's identity is shaped not only by what they inherit, but by culture and experience. So, identity is not created quickly, but constantly shaped, and reshaped, in the context of lived relationships. As we have seen, identity is created and sustained through identification with different groups. For very young children, this occurs most obviously and profoundly in the family and the communities in which they live. The beliefs and practices of the family or religious group help to shape one's character and worldview, though these are not unchanging. For instance, while girls do not necessarily adopt interests or traits associated with femininity, or boys those linked to masculinity, the expectations of family, of the peer group and of society tend to encourage these.

Moral identity requires a sense of agency, the belief or mindset that one can change and be in control of how one acts, at least to some extent. Young children need, right from the start, to build up a sense of agency and identity and to maintain and strengthen this as they move towards adolescence.

And to be engaged, to see the point, and benefit, of why one should act and interact in particular ways.

As we shall see in Chapter 8, young children require boundaries, but adults must work towards explicit, externally set boundaries being needed less and children setting appropriate boundaries for themselves. Otherwise, there is a risk that children will be over-protected and their sense of moral agency insufficiently developed. While too much complexity too soon may lead to confusion, oversimplifying and overprotecting children is likely to lead to dependence and fragility at times of uncertainty.

Character education should involve children practising and developing attributes in a range of situations, with support and reassurance (and where appropriate reprimand) in an environment where anxiety is contained and exploration encouraged. Discernment about how, and when, to exercise these is learned through experience and reflection on experience. For young children such reflection often needs to be guided. A vocabulary of ethics helps children and adults to think about what these attributes entail in practice and to reinforce appropriate, and correct inappropriate, actions, as discussed in Chapter 9. The language of virtues and values provides a suitable basis for such a vocabulary, though the age of the children and the type of setting may mean that some attributes will be given more, others less, emphasis.

What adults emphasize, and how, affects the impact of their feedback. The therapist, Michael White, describes appropriate behaviours and responses being reinforced as 'thickening the narrative'. This might involve saying 'well done for telling me what really happened' to a 3-year-old or 'I appreciated how you looked after Jacob on his first day' to a 9-year-old. Or praising a young child for owning up or including someone who is upset in a game; or an older one for going out of his way to offer help or intervening when someone is being teased. Such positive, and specific, feedback to reinforce children acting in thoughtful and altruistic, even if relatively small, ways helps to thicken the narrative, and so gradually to reshape children's beliefs about themselves and their identity.

Thickening the narrative, over time, provides a defence against the tendency to act impulsively and self-interestedly and external pressures to act in inappropriate ways. Especially with children who are often in trouble, adults must try to find – and focus on – those times when they act thoughtfully or kindly – and so to help create a stronger sense of moral agency. But narrative can be thinned as well as thickened, making a child's sense of identity more fragile. Remember how in Chapter 6 we saw that fear and shame, especially linked to identity, can dent a child's sense of agency and lead to resentment and low self-esteem. A sense of agency and identity is undermined much more easily and quickly than it can be constructed.

This section has outlined some key aspects of how young children's character and moral identity is created and sustained. The next three chapters explore in more detail how adults can support this process.

Part III

Routes into Moral Education

Following the discussion of how young children learn, Part III explores the implications for adults, in influencing children for good, in two senses, encouraging appropriate conduct and over a long period, trying to avoid the pitfalls identified in Chapter 1.

While many of the implications follow logically from the preceding discussion, what is involved is, paradoxically, more complex and simpler than one may think. For instance, adult praise can help to support a sense of moral identity, but some sorts may undermine it. And, while what is described may seem daunting, much of what matters most, like setting a good example, is not as complicated as it may seem.

There is no one route through the rocky terrain which children and adults have to negotiate, so that adults must exercise judgement rather than just follow the manual. These three chapters argue for an approach to character education, broadly interpreted, based on an ethic of care and virtue ethics and running through the whole of children's lives and how any setting operates, as far as possible.

Since learning is reciprocal, it is neither easy, nor helpful, to separate what is involved into neat compartments. So, themes such as language and stories, feedback and example, beliefs and expectations will keep reappearing. However, Chapter 8 discusses the importance, and nature, of inclusive learning environments and Chapter 9 how attributes such as empathy and thoughtfulness can best be cultivated, in the belief that an ethic of care provides an essential foundation for the education of the whole child. Chapter 10, recognizing the challenges which moral educators face in the current climate, emphasizes the need to work in partnership and for personal and institutional authenticity.

Part III

Routes into Moral Education

8

Inclusive Learning Environments

The influence of learning environments

Parker Palmer (1983; 1993, pp. 71–5) suggests that an authentic learning space has three essential dimensions: 'openness, boundaries and an air of hospitality'. Palmer indicates that the openness of a space involves a lack of clutter and is 'created by the firmness of its boundaries', a structure for learning, not 'an invitation to confusion and chaos'(p. 72); and describes hospitality as 'receiving each other, our struggles, our newborn ideas, with openness and care' (p. 74). This section explores why learning environments matter so much and the next two the idea of hospitable space and boundaries, respectively.

As the Rumbold report on early years education states:

> the educator working with under fives must pay careful attention not just to the content of the child's learning, but also to the way in which that learning

is offered to and experienced by the child, and the role of all those involved in the process. Children are affected by the context in which learning takes place, the people involved in it and the values and beliefs which are embedded in it. (DES, 1990, p. 9)

Let us think why this is true for those who work with older children as well, particularly in learning to act and interact appropriately.

An environment is a culture with different interlinked elements – among them physical, emotional, relational and moral. Just as plants put down roots but depend on the right conditions and being cared for if they are to flourish, how children develop depends on the environment in which they grow. In a culture where school learning, and academic success, are not highly valued, it is hard to 'swim against the stream'. No less so, where respect or honesty are not encouraged. Attributes and dispositions may be to some extent inherent but they still require cultivation. As Bloom suggests (2013, p. 119), 'we start off prepared to make distinctions (between people), but it's our environments that tell us precisely how to do so'.

How character is shaped is often seen in individual terms, but an inclusive environment helps to make this a more collective endeavour. The journey is both an individual one and informed by involvement in social and relational networks. Developing a sense of agency and engagement collectively is both easier and more influential in abstract areas such as ethics and morality.

'Childhood is when human beings are initiated into moral communities' (Wall 2010, p. 70). The groups to which we belong help to create and sustain how our ethical lives develop – for better or worse. The environment where one first learns to do something affects long-term attitudes. The family is the milieu in which very young children learn to belong, based on shared beliefs, ways of working and collective expectations. With age, children learn to be part of more, and more diverse, groups; and the peer group and wider cultural influences become increasingly influential. As discussed in Chapter 3, the wider social and cultural environment provides attractive, powerful and often confusing messages and examples. Many children are unsure where they belong and the world offers many attractive but superficial ways of belonging – or at least seeming to.

Environments help define and exemplify how one should conduct oneself, in the short- and the long term. An atmosphere of trust and respect tends to instil habits of trust and respect. A calm, reflective environment encourages and enables those in it to conduct themselves calmly and reflectively; and a caring one to act in caring ways. Children are more likely to be adventurous and imaginative where exploration and imagination is encouraged. Whether conformity, competition or creativity is expected will influence how compliant, competitive or creative they become. So adult expectations help to shape how children conduct themselves, for good or ill.

Dewey (1916, p. 17) wrote: 'while th(e) "unconscious influence of the environment" is so subtle and pervasive that it affects every fiber of character and mind, it may be worthwhile to specify a few directions in which its effect is most marked'. Dewey cites 'the habits of language', manners, good taste and aesthetic appreciation, continuing (p. 18),

> example is notoriously more potent than precept. Good manners come . . . from good breeding or rather are good breeding; and breeding is acquired by habitual action, in response to habitual stimuli, not by conveying information. Despite the never ending play of conscious correction and instruction, the surrounding atmosphere and spirit is in the end the chief agent in forming manners. And manners are but minor morals. Moreover, in major morals, conscious instruction is likely to be efficacious only in the degree in which it falls in with the general 'walk and conversation' of those who constitute the child's social environment.

While the language is old-fashioned, this passage contains two valuable insights:

- the emphasis on example, habituation and the environment in developing a sense of 'that is how we do things here' – by immersion rather than instruction; and
- the link between manners and morals. Much of what Dewey calls good breeding depends on small actions, like asking politely or being interested in other people. Such 'minor morals', or what I call 'small steps', are the basis of learning to act and interact appropriately. So, children should practise 'minor morals' in ordinary situations; and benefit from the chance, and encouragement, to exercise these in different contexts, taking (an increasing level of) responsibility for how they act.

Jackson et al. (1993) worked with a group of teachers (of different age groups) for two-and-a-half years to explore what most influenced moral development. They concluded that all that happens in classrooms affects how and what children learn; and that this is intimately tied up with what adults, often unconsciously, deem worthwhile. So, the quality, availability and accessibility, of books, paint or equipment or how the outdoor environment is used, sends a message about the value ascribed to these. Whether a class sit in rows, or on the floor, or in different groupings is not simply a matter of convenience. Where the teacher stands, or sits, and how she treats children's work, is indicative of, and helps shape, assumptions about what matters and the types of response expected.

Jackson et al. saw direct programmes of moral instruction as less influential than unspoken messages, many of them implicit and subtle. Such messages are often described in words such as ethos or climate, related to how people act and interact and the types of relationship formed and built up over time. In schools, these are part of the 'hidden curriculum'. The formal curriculum is what is taught explicitly; and the informal what takes place outside the classroom, in breaks between lessons and 'extra-curricular' activities. The hidden curriculum is more like the messages, beliefs and values embedded in the DNA of a class, school or other group.

Case study – the hidden curriculum

Even very young children – and maybe they in particular – pick up subtle, unspoken messages about learning and what is expected. I recall a conversation with two parents when Mark's father recounted how they would unsuccessfully quiz him, as a 5-year-old, about what he had learned that day. With a chuckle, he recalled how Mark, exasperated, had finally said to them 'you don't understand, it's not that sort of school'.

Chapter 3 emphasized what Claxton and Carr (2004) called a potentiating environment which strengthens dispositions, by children taking increasing responsibility. As in what Wenger (1998) calls a community of practice, such an environment involves mutual learning and newer members guided by more experienced ones. The experience and knowledge of less experienced learners is respected and their sense of agency encouraged.

In relation to character and ethics, a potentiating environment offers regular opportunities for children to:

- strengthen attributes such as resourcefulness and kindness by practicing them in different, and increasingly demanding, situations;
- broaden their repertoire of such attributes;

- recognize, and practise, how best to apply (possibly conflicting) virtues depending on the context; and
- receive support and reassurance (and where appropriate reprimand) in a secure climate where their sense of moral identity is enriched and thickened.

An environment which enables respectful, reciprocal and purposeful discussion is essential. Everyone must feel able to articulate their ideas and not be afraid of being laughed at or humiliated. Factors such as the group size, the age and background of the children will affect the detail of what this involves, but establishing such an environment requires collective expectations, such as that:

- everyone will try to listen and build on other people's ideas;
- it is alright to express one's view, but one does not have to do so;
- one does not have to agree, but if not must do so respectfully;
- good questions are at least as important as answers.

In particular, appropriate actions are modelled and reinforced and others corrected – by adults and children alike – and a sense of collective agency created and sustained. Such an environment matters for all children, but particularly for who do not have these opportunities elsewhere.

How children learn to conduct themselves is affected both by the (longer-term) climate and the (immediate) mood. These are areas over which individual adults have considerable influence. Parents/carers can establish the climate of security and care which young children need; and help children manage the inevitable ups and downs of life. Individual teachers cannot create system-change, and can usually have only a small influence on children's experience out of school, but can help create an inclusive and enabling learning environment.

With very young children, and those who find self-regulation hard, the mood, and consequently the behaviour, of a group, can change very rapidly, often as a result of one incident or response. Managing the mood of a group in a way which maintains the children's sense of agency but avoids confusion and chaos involves adults remaining in control, but without over-controlling. Working with a group one knows well and who are used to working independently may require less external discipline, while an activity which could be dangerous or chaotic calls for stricter boundaries. So adults must observe carefully, and be attuned to, the group's emotional state – and respond accordingly.

Hospitable space and the moral order

To explore, and practice, how to act and interact appropriately, children – we all – require space. Such space offers the chance to think, to feel, to talk, to listen, to be silent, to play, rather than being dominated by the insistent beat of information, performance and choice, and the stress which accompanies this.

This section explores two ideas:

- hospitable space, recalling Palmer's call for an 'air of hospitality', and discussed in more detail in Eaude (2014); and
- the moral order, where each individual is included and cared for and learns to care for others.

Nouwen (1996) suggests that the word 'hospitable' has its root in the relationship between host and guest, with the host welcoming and the guest welcomed. The guest is someone with specific needs to be considered. He (p. 69) writes 'hospitality is not to change people, but to offer them space where change can take place'. The chance to change is offered rather than forced. Nouwen continues that 'someone who is filled with ideas, concepts, opinions and convictions cannot be a good host. There is no inner space to listen, no openness to discover the gift of the other' (p. 96).

For space to be hospitable implies that the relationship between host and guest(s) is reciprocal and non-coercive and the benefit mutual, though not necessarily evenly so. Hospitable space enables those within it to explore and think about their feelings and actions, in ways that may be impossible when stressed. Children who are least experienced and resilient as learners are those who most need hospitable space.

Hospitable space provides opportunities for everyone, whatever their previous experience, religion or background, to:

- be recognized, accepted and cared-for;
- fit in and belong;
- reflect, imagine and explore what concerns them.

If children are to explore – rather than just be told – how to act and interact appropriately, the environment needs to be hospitable. And there must be opportunities for everyone to express their ideas – and sometimes to be silent – without fear of ridicule or their views being dismissed.

Silence often helps to calm children who are agitated or excited and to encourage reflection. But silence can feel threatening when one is anxious or unused to it. Sitting silently as a group may be unnerving until everyone is used to doing so. So, creating hospitable space involves containing anxiety by establishing boundaries within which children feel safe, and so able to explore.

Some, mostly older, children may wish to think about and discuss big, existential, ethical questions and can do so profoundly, especially when they are emotionally engaged. Consider the following example.

Case study – freedom or safety?

I vividly recall a discussion with a class of 9-year-olds about the rights and wrongs of zoos. At one point, Brenda, quiet but forceful, said 'I think that zoos are wrong because freedom is always more important than comfort'. It was not Neil's turn to speak but he could not contain himself. 'I don't agree with Brenda', he said, 'you'd rather be secure with your mum even if you were enslaved.' The rest of the class, and I, listened, transfixed, as they debated, without coming to any conclusion, one of the oldest, most profound arguments in philosophy.

For such discussion to be reciprocal requires careful listening and responding respectfully to other people's views and questions; and for it to be purposeful, it has to be steered. The adult's role is to steer discussion and to model thinking processes, applying rules flexibly where appropriate. For instance, a strict emphasis on turn-taking would have made this discussion impossible. So, creating an environment where children can talk and think together about such issues requires collective expectations, built up over time, but interpreted flexibly.

However, young children's concerns are much more likely to be about everyday questions such as how brave to be, and how to be brave, when faced by a bully or whether to be kind to someone who is unkind to you. Chapter 9 discusses further how adults can help children to think about these.

Nouwen (1996, p. 80) asks 'is it possible to become hospitable to each other in a classroom?' continuing that 'it is far from easy since both teachers and students are part of a very demanding, pushing and often exploitative society in which . . . schools no longer have the time or space where the questions about why we live and love, work and die can be raised without fear of competition, rivalry or concern about punishments and rewards'. So, creating hospitable space is not easy in formal institutions, such as schools, in the current climate.

Mayall (2010, pp. 66–7) argues that variations in children's achievement may be profoundly rooted in the school's social attitudes, emphasizing that schools have a pivotal role in providing a counter to the often-confusing world which children inhabit. In Eaude (2007), I described schools as 'beacons of hope for those adrift in a sea of uncertainty'. I am now less sure, but remain convinced that many schools and settings, particularly for young children, provide inspiring examples of what Mayall calls the 'moral order'.

The moral order enables those within it to experience how to live a life where how one acts and interacts matters, without imposing too definite a template of what this entails. How the moral order is manifested in practice must take account of factors such as the children's age, prior experience and cultural and religious backgrounds. But it is necessarily inclusive (at least of those within it). To belong is easier if you already, to some extent, feel that you belong, making it particularly important that those who are, or feel themselves to be, outsiders are welcomed. Those who may easily be excluded, or are at risk of being so, are not only those with disabilities and from ethnic and linguistic minorities, but also those whose voices often remain unheard – those who are least educated, those whose lives are blighted by poverty and children themselves. Remember how Wall argues that children are often systematically excluded, and rarely receive a proper hearing, in a world dominated by consumer or parental choice, where those who shout loudest are heard most clearly. So, the moral order implies an environment where adults listen to, and take account of, all children's voices.

The moral order involves adults attending to the ideas, funds of knowledge and insights that children bring, including those most likely to be excluded otherwise. Incorporation into, and experience of, the moral order helps everyone, particularly those from backgrounds which may make them less resilient – as a result of factors such as neglect, racism or discrimination – and those who do not encounter such an environment elsewhere. By helping to protect those who may otherwise be excluded and providing an example to those who may be inclined to exclude others, the moral order encourages inclusiveness, entitlement and awareness of, and attention to, other people's needs.

Inclusion is often used only to mean those with disabilities being educated in the same setting as others, but as Graham and Slee (2008, p. 278) indicate, 'to include is not necessarily to *be* inclusive'. Exclusion can work in subtle ways. The moral order implies a deeper view of inclusion where:

- individuals are attended and listened to, and their knowledge and experience respected, whatever their age, ability or background;
- unkindness and discrimination is challenged; and
- expectations are high but realistic.

We shall discuss expectations in more detail. However, let us consider the implications of the first two points in relation to ethics. We all, but young children especially, need to be loved and cared-for, as individuals, with our joys shared and celebrated and our worries listened and attended to. And children – we all – need to care for, to attend and listen to, others, if we are not to be caught up with our own concerns.

An ethic of care does not mean that children should not be challenged. Indeed, care involves challenge. So, for instance, overcoming difficulties is necessary to help build resilience, so that activities should take children outside their comfort zone, though not too far. And if we are to avoid a sense that 'anything goes' adults must be prepared to challenge comments and behaviours, especially anti-social ones which upset or hurt other people and undermine expectations of what is acceptable.

Nussbaum (2010, pp. 43–4) argues that structures become pernicious when:

- those involved are not personally accountable for their actions;
- no one raises a critical voice against wrong-doing; and
- those who are less powerful are dehumanized and de-individualized.

If children (and adults) are not expected to consider the consequences of their actions, and inappropriate behaviour goes unchallenged, then anything goes and the moral order starts to crumble.

Let us think what this might entail in practice when working with young children. It may often seem easier to ignore hurtful comments or small unkindnesses, especially with children who may not realize the impact of their comments or actions. But small actions matter. So, asserting the moral order implies that racist, homophobic or other hurtful comments are not allowed to pass unchallenged, particularly when these refer to aspects of cultural identity or are directed towards the most vulnerable and least powerful. But adults must be sensitive to how best to do so. For instance, it may be best to challenge unkind behaviour in general terms in public, but to address specific incidents separately with one particular child or group. Those least able to regulate their conduct need to be nurtured not lectured, supported not shamed. And public confrontation rarely benefits anyone. Chapter 9 discusses in more detail the role of language in reinforcing good, and challenging bad, behaviour.

Over time, challenging inappropriate behaviour must become not just the adults' responsibility, but everyone's. With very young children, this may entail adults praising those who act thoughtfully when they do not have to, so encouraging other children to do so; and with 9- or 10-year-olds, expecting them to take greater responsibility, individually and collectively, for their actions, for instance both in not taking part in bullying and in intervening when it occurs.

Boundaries, routines and rules

Few people would suggest that children do not require the range of choices available to them to be restricted. Indeed, this is an essential part of adults' responsibilities. So, it would be ridiculous to allow a young child to take another person's property or to push someone over without, at the least, indicating that this is inappropriate and seeking to alter such behaviour in the future.

Setting such boundaries helps establish the parameters of acceptable conduct; but children also need opportunities to test out whether, and in which circumstances, such expectations apply. Many actions appropriate in a playground or at a party are not in a place of worship; and the conduct encouraged at home and school may differ. Think of the toddler who does something naughty and then looks to see her parents' response; or of the 10-year-old who makes a provocative remark and awaits the response of those around him. Both are, in different ways, testing the boundaries of social acceptability. Boundaries provide the openness for exploration, as long as they are not too restrictive. So, adults must establish boundaries, but, as we shall see, judge how flexible and porous these should be.

Routines, such as bed-time stories and meals, help to provide security at home. In more formal settings, the welcome at the start, and saying goodbye at the end, of the day and gathering for a story or a prayer help to define what it means to be part of a group and make individuals feel part of it. These routines are simple, but significant, ways of building relationships and establishing expectations. As well as providing predictability and security, such routines help to settle children as they move into a new context and to reassure them as they prepare to move on. Such routines and relationships matter especially for children who are least sure or resilient and those who lead fragmented or chaotic lives. But routines can easily become routinized, tedious or constraining, over time. So, while adults need to maintain such routines, it is helpful to refresh them and look for different ways in which they are carried out, for instance by children being involved in how they are designed, adapted and led.

What is expected and acceptable is often made public in the form of rules, codes of conduct or a list of shared values. Young children tend to think of rules in terms of what is prohibited rather than encouraged and so may need help to frame them in positive terms. I have suggested that these should emphasize specific attributes and types of behaviour to be encouraged, but not presented as universal or to be applied without thought. Importantly, expectations, that 'this is how we conduct ourselves here', must apply to everyone if adults are to avoid hypocrisy.

While it usually helps if adults make such expectations explicit, and refer to them regularly, doing so too often can disengage those who have 'heard it all before'. We internalize best when ideas are presented, and experience is represented, in several modes. So, one needs to find a variety of ways to exemplify expectations, not just in words, but by displays and symbols, especially those designed and created by children.

Adults may have to set out (some) clear and non-negotiable rules, for instance in relation to safety and discriminatory behaviour, as discussed above. But children are more likely to understand and abide by rules they have devised; and which they are collectively responsible for enforcing. At the least, rules should be open to discussion, debate and revision, if children are to understand the rationale behind, and be motivated to abide by, them; and the resultant behaviours not to be based on unthinking compliance.

In some circumstances, especially when children are less used to exercising judgement about what is appropriate given the context, clear boundaries and expectations may be necessary. However, this must always be with a view to encouraging children to think 'why', recognize the consequences of their actions and consider alternative possibilities. Such an approach helps to wean children from dependence on adults and so to develop their judgement and narrative of the sort of person they wish to become.

Simple, non-negotiable rules such as 'always ask before borrowing something' or 'wait until the other person has stopped speaking before you do' may be helpful, especially with very young children or those who find conscious choices difficult. But more general maxims, such as 'treat others as you would like them to treat you' or 'leave this place as you would wish to find it' encourage discernment and guide action while taking account of the messiness of what the world is like.

Less specific than rules, maxims help to guide conduct rather than pre-scribe behaviour and are likely to be more influential in the long term. Such maxims may be drawn from religious or secular sources, but their strength lies in their generality and encouragement to consider the context and other people. These reflect, and help shape, a view that correct action often involves conflicting demands and that rules should not be applied regardless of context. Making such maxims explicit, and referring to them in considering specific dilemmas or incidents, helps children think how to apply them and adults, including those not present, to reinforce or correct children's actions.

How rules are interpreted and applied matters even more than how they are formulated. Adults are expected not only to apply rules fairly and con-sistently, but also to differentiate according to varying needs. Children used to predictable responses are more able to cope with uncertainty and anxi-ety; and those who live chaotic lives are likely to require more explicit, and inflexibly applied, boundaries. Otherwise, such children's anxiety may be heightened even further. This highlights a dilemma when working with large and diverse groups, in deciding the balance to be struck between pre-senting a common set of expectations and responding sensitively to those with different beliefs and expectations.

Consistent responses help most children understand the relationship between their choices and the consequences. But adults must moderate this and exercise judgement, using their knowledge of individuals and their prior experience, rather than adopt a one-size-fits-all approach. For exam-ple, a comment seen as cheeky might be intended as questioning; and a child who pushes another may be acting in a friendly way or aggressively. So, rules must be interpreted and applied fairly and predictably but with sufficient flexibility and compassion to allow for children's intentions, as well as their actions, to be considered.

Expecting rules to be applied unbendingly discourages children from making judgements. However, when adult responses seem – or are – incon-sistent, adults should explain, and if need be, justify their actions. For instance, there may be times when rules which a whole group sees as apply-ing to everyone are suspended for some individuals; or when promises given cannot be fulfilled. In such cases, children's trust may be undermined unless adults explain why; and such discussion helps to model the thinking processes behind making difficult choices when the appropriate course of action is not obvious.

The most important expectations are often implicit, more like conventions or 'how-we-do-things-here', such as saying please and thank you or not snatching what one wants. Such implicit rules may not obvious to those in an unfamiliar environment. The idea of cultural capital helps to explain why. Put simply, this relates to how familiar the individual is with the environment and its implicit rules or messages. It may help to think of situations where you feel 'at home' or uneasy. I know better how to act appropriately in a meeting than at a disco. You may feel at ease, or not, at a loud party, in a place of worship or a foreign country. These feelings are largely about whether you fit in. Cultural capital may be compared with money, where coins which have value in one place do not in another; or where someone not fluent in a language picks up only some of the intended messages.

Children from a home where sharing their toys or talking about the impact of their actions is encouraged tend to be at an advantage in school settings; and those for whom the messages about how to act and interact which they hear at home and at school do not match may find the expectations confusing. For instance, when a parent says to hit back when provoked and the teacher not to, the child may not know how to react; and where a young Muslim girl has been taught at home to be modest, but is expected to undress publicly to change, she may become anxious.

Learning new expectations, many of which are unspoken, requires additional support and takes time. Teachers may have to explain unfamiliar ideas even more clearly to a young bilingual learner than a native speaker, without lowering the cognitive level. Similarly, adults may need to be more explicit with those who are unfamiliar with, or confused about, how to conduct themselves, but without lowering expectations. Such explicit support helps to reduce for both children and families the danger of confusion – and the anxiety likely to accompany this.

Working across all subject areas

In this section, we consider in more detail how every aspect of education has a moral dimension and why attributes associated with character and ethics need to be cultivated across, and beyond, all subject areas.

Case study- two girls temporarily transformed

In a boisterous class of 10- and 11-year-olds, we had watched a series of TV programmes about the eighteenth century, with children acting different roles in small groups. Two very quiet girls rarely got animated, in whatever group or role they were. One week, I heard a tremendous commotion, with banging on the table and shouting. Curbing my desire to intervene, I watched and listened to these two. The whole class stopped, riveted, as the two girls were transformed into peasant women refusing to allow themselves and their families to be turfed out of their houses for not paying the rent. Suddenly, they paused, looked embarrassed and resumed their more usual identity.

This incident could have occurred in a history, or drama, or personal and social education lesson. Wherever it occurred in the formal curriculum, the two girls were learning much more than a subject, but about themselves and people in the past and how one might respond to distress and injustice.

Moral education is often seen as taking place mainly in specific subjects, lessons and programmes. In England, these may be called Personal, Social and Health and Citizenship Education (PSHCE) and Religious Education. In other countries, such lessons may be called by various names including social studies, civics and character education.

In schools, assemblies are usually seen an important forum to affirm, explore and reinforce expectations, particularly in relation to behaviour. In classrooms, and many settings out of school, formal times where the class or group gathers provides an opportunity for a reminder about what is expected, to sort out difficulties and to reflect on what has gone well.

Having timetabled slots where moral and ethical issues are explicitly addressed provides space within an often-crowded curriculum, making an explicit statement that these matter. Without these, there is a risk that the moral dimension of education will be overlooked. However, the danger is that moral education too easily comes to be seen as the domain of only certain subjects or separate programmes, the limitations of which are discussed in Chapter 10.

In recent years, programmes based on games and discussion in groups, often using circle time, to develop what Goleman (1996) calls emotional intelligence (EI), have become popular. As indicated in Claxton (2005, pp. 8–9), EI as a concept has expanded to include just about everything apart from traditional academic concerns and analytical thinking. More worryingly, Ecclestone and Hayes (2008) argue that an emphasis on feelings rather than knowledge tends to encourage a sense of dependence and vulnerability rather than agency and resilience. They write (p. 145) 'the development of emotional literacy and the "skills" associated with emotional well-being begins children's preoccupation with themselves, introduces the idea that life makes us vulnerable and offer prescriptive rituals, scripts and appropriate ways of behaving emotionally'.

Ecclestone and Hayes suggest that such approaches discourage children from engaging with the complexity and ambiguity of emotional responses and learning to cope with difficulty. This reflects Scheindlin's (2003, p. 187) view that the dominant theme of Goleman's work on emotional intelligence, and approaches based on it, is the management and control of emotions, rather than developing the capacity to express a range of different emotions. Such approaches tend to overlook the differences in children and the circumstances of their lives. While programmes to develop social and emotional skills can be helpful, this process needs to happen across the whole range of children's lives.

Education cannot be value-free, but neither can it be content-free. Knowledge, skills and understanding are inextricably linked, with each other and with identity and character. In Dewey's words, teachers need to 'teach all subjects in such a way as to bring out their social and personal aspects, stressing how human beings are affected by them, pointing up the responsibilities that flow from their interrelatedness' (see Noddings 2013, p. 179). A moral dimension should permeate the whole formal curriculum – and beyond.

Mathematics and science may seem largely technical rather than ethical subjects, to do with propositional, content knowledge. But mathematical problems can be set to explore questions of equity or population change and science presents moral dilemmas, for example to do with the environment and climate change or genetically modified crops. While such topics are likely to be of more interest to children from the age of about 9 upwards, they may fascinate younger children when raised in context.

Literature, the humanities and the arts provide similar opportunities. Fiction and poetry frequently encourage listeners and readers to see and feel the world in new ways, raising questions of motivation and morality. History raises many overtly moral questions, for example whether, and when, war is justified or those related to slavery or Nazism. Geography provides opportunities to consider different people and cultures and issues such as the reasons for migration or why the world contains so many people who are overfed while so many go hungry. These enable children (to some extent) to understand and empathize with people separated from themselves by time and space; and to learn about similarity and difference, across time and culture.

However, any subject has both a specific ethical aspect and a more general contribution to character education. Take the example of Physical Education (PE). Traditionally, team sport was considered to develop character by people learning to abide by the rules, overcome difficulties and win and lose gracefully. PE provides obvious opportunities to take turns, be aware of other people's abilities and needs and work in teams, for instance in performing a dance. Its practical nature is particularly useful to help children to see and to enact what cooperation and trust involve in practice. So, while there is an overtly ethical aspect to PE, no less important is how it helps to develop attributes associated with acting and interacting appropriately.

So, consideration of overtly moral issues *can* happen in any subject area, though opportunities are more obvious in some than others. But this misses the essential point that moral education is more like a process, or way of working, embedded within each subject and across the curriculum, than a question of content. The attributes and dispositions associated with character and ethics not only can, but must, be developed throughout the life of the setting. This is one main reason why it helps to think of character education as an overall approach, not a separate subject.

Let us think through the implications. Since many of the most important opportunities occur in small, unforeseen interactions, rather than being planned in advance, planning must be flexible to create and respond situations where such opportunities arise. When one teacher is with a class for much of the week, the moral dimension can be addressed during, or as a result of any activity and in any subject area, either at the time or subsequently. With very young children, how the curriculum is usually structured offers more scope for crossing subject boundaries, providing a flexibility not available with a rigidly structured timetable.

Young children learn primarily, and most deeply, through activity and using varied, mutually supportive, ways of representing experience, rather than abstract, decontextualized thought. While language can act as a prompt or a reminder, children – we all – have to experience what such ways of working feel like rather than just knowing the words. For instance, one gains the procedural knowledge associated with being a scientist by processes such as hypothesizing and experimenting or a historian by searching for and interpreting clues. Similarly, one learns to work cooperatively and thoughtfully by doing so and to become fair, or respectful, by acting regularly in those ways.

Aptitudes and talents will not become apparent without the chance to try a wide range of activities and experiences. So, children require a breadth of opportunities if they are to be engaged and to work both independently and cooperatively. To develop resilience, children must learn to cope with challenge and adversity. To become more empathetic, one must come to see the world from other people's perspectives, those who are different as well as those who are similar. To become more compassionate, children need chances to care-for other sentient beings, both people and pets, if they are to develop a sense of responsibility and understand how others feel and respond. While dolls and plants are not sentient beings, the opportunity to look after them provides a route into taking responsibility for something other than oneself.

Such attributes are not learned only in lessons planned to encourage these but in how children are encouraged to work in groups, to hold discussions or to resolve difficulties. All of these processes require time, space and guidance rather than pressure, pace and instruction. We have seen that children need an inclusive environment which is caring, safe and predictable, but not too soft, protective and inflexible. Chapter 10 returns to how to balance conflicting priorities. While moral education does not happen only in some subject areas, some activities and experiences offer particular fertile opportunities for developing empathy and thoughtfulness; and so providing the foundation of ethical action. So, Chapter 9 considers the types of experience, activity and response which help to develop such attributes.

Encouraging Empathy and Thoughtfulness

Play, playfulness and drama

This chapter considers the types of activity, experience and response most likely to encourage attributes such as empathy and thoughtfulness.

You may, immediately, think that play and playfulness has little or nothing to do with the serious business of moral education. In most industrial countries, play is usually considered – as in my childhood – a somewhat frivolous activity, the opposite of work, which children should grow out of. Such a view contains three assumptions to be challenged, that play is just an activity, not serious and only for children.

Play is both an activity and a process. One of a baby's most basic activities is to play, as a way of making sense of their relationship with the people, things and environment they encounter. While primarily associated with childhood, play remains important in many adults' lives, for example in sport, or music, or acting. However, such playing is usually more structured and rule-bound than children's play; and (usually) linked to leisure, something peripheral to, or in contrast to, the world of work, with real learning supposedly taking place only when we 'work at it'.

These assumptions, inevitably, affect how we view play. Think, for example, of how most schools separate work, structurally, from playtime or recess; and how some have a 'golden time' when children, having completed their (serious) work, have a chance to play. Play is implicitly looked down on by many adults. For young children, play *is* work, until they are taught otherwise. Consider Winnicott's (2002, p. 54) words, 'it is in playing and only in playing that the individual child or adult is able to be creative and to use the whole personality, and it is only in being creative that the individual discovers the self'.

Finding a satisfactory definition of play is hard because the term covers many types of activity and process. McMahon (1992, p. 1) describes play as 'a spontaneous and active process in which thinking, feeling and doing can flourish since they are separated from the fear of failure or disastrous consequences'. One fundamental feature is that people and things can assume, or be given, different identities. So, a stick can become a magic wand, a conductor's baton or a gun. A timid girl can become a princess or a dragon and a macho boy dress as his grandma or a wolf. One can operate with the meaning of something detached from what it appears to be, or is, in reality. This fluidity helps children to develop a sense of agency and to explore their own and other people's feelings and responses in safe space.

Tassoni and Hucker (2005, p. 9) characterize five stages of play – solitary, spectator, parallel, associative and cooperative – whereby individuals learn about, and practice, relationships with increasing levels of interaction and cooperation. In Siraj-Blatchford's (1999, p. 29) words, 'Piaget argued that reciprocity in peer relations provides the foundations for perspective taking and for decentring. This suggests that collaborative play is exceptionally important for children.' Play offers an unforced way from individual to socialized activity and enables reciprocal relationships in an uncontrolling and unthreatening way, encouraging empathy and cooperation.

Play supports conceptual development and metacognition, since in Vygotsky's (1978, p. 97) words, 'action according to rules begins to be determined by ideas and not the objects themselves'. Play helps the child to move towards more general and abstract thinking, but in a way where s/he remains in control. In play, the individual, however small or insignificant, can experiment and explore, without having to take the consequences, especially the emotional ones, of failure. So, play provides space to take risks safely.

As Nussbaum (2010, p. 101) writes, 'play teaches people to be capable of living with others without control; it connects experiences of vulnerability and surprise to curiosity and wonder, rather than to crippling anxiety'. For some children, especially those who are feeling most insecure or anxious, play may be the only way of enabling this. I vividly recall how a 6-year-old who had experienced considerable trauma could not talk about it, but was able to start reliving it through play, and so begin to come to terms with his worries, in a way that was impossible through language. Of course, such a process often requires sensitive, specialized support.

Hyde (2009) warns against what he calls pseudoplay, particularly dangerous since it disguises itself as play, with its features being that participation is:

- required rather than inherently pleasurable;
- based on predetermined learning outcomes rather than engaged in for its own sake;
- directed rather than spontaneous;
- passive rather than requiring engagement.

Hyde identifies four types of danger in pseudoplay:

- compulsion, misusing power to take control of the activity and the outcome;
- entertainment, making children into passive consumers;
- manipulation, exerting undue influence; and
- competition, since making meaning is inherently non-competitive and for every winner there are losers.

These echo several pitfalls identified in Chapter 1. While play is essential in children gaining a sense of self, adults must be careful not to misuse it or to overdirect its outcomes.

Even when the benefit of young children playing is (partly) recognized, the importance of qualities such as playfulness and humour are often overlooked, particularly with older children. Inventors, artists and authors frequently attest that being playful with alternative possibilities, divergent, not over-focused on immediate results is essential in the creative process: whether composing a picture or a piece of music, writing a story or poem or deciding how to respond to uncertainty.

Playfulness can not only make learning more enjoyable but steer it into new areas, building on children's interests rather than just what adults prescribe or plan. Playfulness can help children imagine new possibilities, for the world to be other than it appears. Since it is a process, a way of approaching a task, playfulness can happen in any domain of learning, given the right environment and encouragement, though it is easier in some than others.

Ethics is a serious business, but this does not mean that one should be humourless or po-faced about it. For instance, when thinking together what it means to be kind, thoughtful or patient (or otherwise), silly or funny examples, such as cartoon characters or using a glove puppet, may help young children understand these ideas far better than a lecture. However, there is no place for sarcasm in a caring, inclusive learning environment.

Drama, like play, enables one to explore safely how identity can be altered temporarily, how it is to feel and to see the world 'as if' from another person's perspective. It is no coincidence that one talks of characters in drama, since these are alternative constructions of people who, while not real, might be. Whether as participant or watcher (though watchers are also participants), drama has the potential to help one to understand the world from other perspectives; and so to move from focusing primarily on oneself and develop empathy for how other people feel. Both play and drama help children to embody their feelings and articulate their responses in ways which include both unconscious and conscious learning mechanisms. Because drama is specific, active and interactive (see Winston, 1998, p. 46), it enables even young children to process emotion, both their own and other people's, without relying too heavily, or possibly at all, on language and other conscious processes.

Think back to the incident of the two girls acting as dispossessed peasants described in the last chapter. One can never know how such an experience affected those two girls, or those watching, in the long term. However, the emotional intensity suggests that they gained a much deeper understanding of how it was to live 200 years ago than any factual description could have provided. Drama provides the chance to adopt, and try out, different identities and narratives of who one is or might be; to imagine and act out how it is to be someone else, at least for a time, and so understand and empathize to some extent how one, and other people, may feel and respond in different ways. Drama enables one to enter an imagined world and to explore and recreate a narrative of oneself. In different but related ways, the same is true of stories.

Stories

Stories may seem more obviously linked to moral education than play does. For example, the stories of faith are central to most religious traditions, from those told about Abraham and Mohammed to those used by Jesus and the Buddha. Stories have been used to pass on profound religious and cultural truths. And many stories have a 'moral', a message about the right course of action. But this section suggests that stories fulfil a more fundamental role in helping create moral identity.

To listen to a story may seem just an enjoyable activity, which encourages careful listening. Stories often help illustrate a point and hearing or reading them provides an enjoyable route into alternative realities. But there is far more to stories than this. Cupitt (1995) suggests that we all, throughout life, constantly seek to create new narratives which describe our lives more appropriately than previous ones. He (1995, p. ix) writes '(stories) shape the process of life. It is through stories that our social selves, which are our real selves, are actually produced'.

Bruner (1996, p. 147) suggests, we live in 'a sea of stories' which paradoxically makes it hard to see how they operate. So, let us think why stories, told or read well, work at a deeper and subtler level.

First, stories are enjoyable and accessible. They do not make direct demands of the listener, but help us to understand experience, both our own and other people's, and to integrate the two. Because most good stories are about choices and dilemmas, they provide an engaging and unthreatening route into reflection on these. Their open-endedness and provisionality, and how they raise questions about how one should act, help to introduce complex issues in suggestive rather than prescriptive ways. Well-told stories enable one to cope with mystery and ambiguity, since as Arendt (1970, p. 105) wrote, 'storytelling reveals meaning without committing the error of defining it'. For example, one of the earliest incidents in the Bible is where Cain has killed his brother, Abel, and is asked by God if he knows where Abel is. Cain asks 'Am I my brother's keeper?' This question, left hanging, prompts hearers to reflect on the extent of our responsibility to other people. For a 6-year-old, this might be to what extent she should be kind to those who are not her friends and for a 10-year-old to what extent we bear responsibility for those less well-off than ourselves, whether in our community or on the other side of the world.

Second, good stories are open-ended. They allow for alternative possibilities and courses of action, though most stories reach a conclusion, where the questions are resolved, at least provisionally. As Erricker (1998, p. 109) indicates, 'real stories by virtue of being lived are necessarily unfinished and beg questions rather than provide answers . . . They involve a continual remembering of the story itself'. So, stories suggest and resonate, rather than preach, when told well, because they bear repeated retelling by both teller and listener. In Winston's (1998, p. 21) words, 'stories . . . inform our choices in life, they do not dictate them', helping to guide children in the struggle to understand, and shape, their own identity, their place in the wider scheme of things.

Third, as Anning (1997, p. 9) writes, 'for children the function of narrative can be to enable them to move from the here and now of their immediate experiences to the more distanced ideas about what happened then and what might happen next. In other words, the narrative form is a potent resource to help children move to abstractions.' Stories, therefore, help to link the child's own experience to more abstract, general ideas – and vice versa – reaching beyond their immediate reality. In Kimes Myers' (1997, p. 18) words, 'story connects us with that which lies beyond ourselves and this process makes us ask questions about the meanings of our lives'.

So, stories are powerful tools for the exploration of beliefs and values. Their open-ended, recreatable, nature helps cultivate the moral imagination and encourage thinking about possible choices in an unthreatening way. Stories help even very young children understand attributes such as courage and patience and develop others such as curiosity, empathy and judgement. For example, the parable of the prodigal son, where the selfish brother returns having squandered his fortune and is welcomed by the father, to the chagrin of the loyal brother who stayed and feels taken for granted, raises questions of justice, love, jealousy and forgiveness without reaching too definite a conclusion.

Fourth, stories link us to other cultures and generations and offer examples of what to do (or otherwise). They are fundamental to understanding history, religion and literature – and so ourselves and other people – providing a framework for linking otherwise disjointed factual knowledge. Stories help us to understand events, and ourselves, as part of a continuity, something bigger than ourselves; and so to define ourselves in relation to others, as part of a constantly changing narrative.

Stories enable us to see ourselves as part of bigger groups and longer traditions, maybe to do with a religion, nationality or ethnicity, countering the tendency to see oneself only as an individual. Stories are essential elements in creating and developing identity. As Wilson (2007, p. 110) writes, 'stories are not ends in themselves . . . (they) create links to other possible stories, looping back and forth in memory and imagination. We retain stories from our families, from our teachers, from literature and popular media including film and theatre. They can carry enduring messages that are personal to us and harbour meaning that only we can know'. So, 'stories learned in childhood become powerful constituents of the world we inhabit as adults' (Nussbaum, 2010, p. 36). It is worth pondering Macintyre's (1999, p. 216) words, 'deprive children of their stories and you leave them unscripted, anxious stutterers in their actions as in their words'. Understanding who one is, and where one fits in, depends on the story that one tells about oneself – whether in words or through other means.

One of the functions of narrative is to hold cognition, emotion and action together and thereby to give meaning to human experience. Narrative provides coherence of meaning to otherwise disparate events, since stories are (usually) about human agents with desires, beliefs, knowledge, intentions and commitments (see Bruner, 1996, chapter 1). We recognize ourselves in other people and other people in ourselves. Hearing and reading stories helps children to retell and enrich their own stories of themselves. For instance, a story such as 'The Very Hungry Caterpillar', apart from being enjoyable, explores how identity changes over time and 'The Gruffalo' helps, in an exciting and amusing way, a young child to realize not only that her fears can be overcome, but how she can participate in this. The Greek myths are not just about heroes and gods long ago, but about universal themes of love and jealousy, honour and deception, courage and betrayal. Stories, whether told or read or seen, help to explore human emotions and experience, actions and interactions.

So, stories work in multiple, subtle, often unconscious, ways, including:

- posing questions to encourage investigation of inference and motivation;
- connecting with other people and cultures;
- helping to provide a language and a space to explore feelings and beliefs where each listener can respond in their own way;
- nurturing the imagination;
- prompting reflection.

Let me add a few words of warning. I have mentioned 'good' stories. There are many wonderful stories both from traditional and recently published sources – of heroes and villains, of different faiths, cultures and communities – along with other ones which preach at, or infantilize, children. So, which stories to use requires judgement and how they are read, or told, matters.

As with play and pseudoplay, adults can easily overcontrol a story's message. Adults are often tempted to read those with a definite 'moral', a lesson to be learned, and so close off, rather extend, reflection (both out loud and in the child's head); and with young children to present stories with a binary view of good and bad and to avoid stories which raise difficult issues. However, fairy stories and those in the Old Testament, for instance, do not shy away from such issues and gather much of their power from this.

Good stories raise questions and allow resonances rather than define solutions. And good story-tellers or story-readers rarely explain a story, but rather allow listeners to come to their own understanding of it. A story is a process, not just an event, with its power being that its meanings are multiple and shaped and reshaped by the listener. As with other tools for moral education, adults should be wary of too much prescription, or moralizing. So, it matters how we use language in encouraging or discouraging particular behaviours – and the next section considers this.

Using language

As Mercer (2000, p. 15) suggests 'language is not simply a system for transmitting, it is a system for thinking collectively'. Language helps to relate local, personal experience to abstract ideas – and vice versa. Words enable half-formed thoughts to be articulated and understanding to be enriched, with more experienced users of language helping to reframe these and add new layers of complexity or nuance.

Words help even very young children to reflect on, and to inform, action. Talking about different ways in which people do, and might, respond, can enable even very young children to think about how they should conduct themselves, though they may have only a naïve understanding of the language. Most children find this easier in spoken than written language, because the former is quicker and less permanent. However, the public nature of spoken language may be more threatening, unless children are confident that those listening will treat their ideas with respect.

Language is an active tool for articulating and so clarifying ideas, which is why young children benefit more from speaking than from listening. However, language is reciprocal so that adults can help to reshape children's understanding by reframing what they say in more precise or complex ways. Discussion helps to articulate, and shape, children's thinking and encourage reflection both on what has happened and what they might have done, or might do, differently.

Using the language of ethics is often associated with formal group discussions such as circle time or Philosophy for Children (P4C). Group discussion can take place in such planned sessions or more on the spur of the moment. Sometimes, adults just need to gather a group to:

- calm down and think how and why a situation got out of hand – and how to put things right and avoid recurrences; and
- work towards a solution, preferably led by the children, for instance an apology or deciding how to support or include a child who has felt excluded.

For dialogue to be reciprocal and cumulative, participants must not have to wait too long before being able to contribute. So, children's engagement is best maintained in small groups. Sitting in a circle or a horseshoe enables everyone to see each other, which encourages careful listening unless individuals prompt each other to act inappropriately. A second adult is often helpful, at least initially, both to discourage this and model attentive and responsive dialogue.

However, talking about how one should act and interact must take place in the normal course of events, not just in formal sessions or large groups. With very young children, this may involve thinking together what patience or cooperation involve; and with older ones, working out how to balance, or resolve conflicts, for instance between being loyal to friends and telling the truth.

A vocabulary of ethics enables children – and adults – to examine, and reflect on, their own and other people's actions and relate these to the attributes and behaviours involved, to explore what the latter entail and see what they look like in practice. As indicated, these attributes will probably include those more specifically related to ethics, such as honesty, compassion, respect and loyalty and more general ones, such as courage, resilience and resourcefulness. But, in practice, I doubt that such a distinction matters that much.

An easily understood vocabulary of ethics is important particularly for very young children and those less used to the conventions of social interaction, as a result of their experience before and outside formal settings. But one difficulty in working with children as they approach adolescence is how to encourage reflection and discussion beyond the very simple level of 'one should tell the truth' or 'do not take other people's property'. As we have seen, different imperatives may conflict; and greater complexity makes clashes between messages from different aspects of children's lives more likely and often more intense.

Just as someone learning a new language must move beyond what is required to meet basic interpersonal needs, a vocabulary of ethics requires increasingly sophisticated usage and a more accurate use of the words, as one encounters greater complexity. Like the vocabulary of geography, science or art, that of ethics needs not only to be related to everyday life but also be increasingly specific about attributes and dispositions to be encouraged. So the language must be used with the guidance of someone more experienced, over time and with regular practice.

Because many of the ideas associated with ethics are abstract, discussion and debate is most formative when referring to real situations and starting from children's experiences and questions. Children must feel able, and be encouraged, to ask difficult or divergent questions, those which they may find hard to raise elsewhere, whether for personal, cultural or other reasons. It is usually easier to think through puzzling or difficult questions with others than doing so alone. Such discussion may end by posing other questions rather than necessarily reaching definite conclusions.

For some, the home may be an ideal place to discuss difficult issues; but, for many, school, or another setting outside the home, may be the best, perhaps the only structured, place to do so. This is easiest with a trusted adult or in a small group, but harder in a large group, where adults tend to dominate discussion and close down children's questioning too quickly; and 'waiting one's turn' stifles real dialogue.

Suppose a 5-year-old has taken something that was not his. For discussion to be formative, this may refer to attributes such as honesty (about owning up) or kindness (in returning the item) and focus on 'next steps' rather just 'telling off'. Or, where an 11-year-old has had to decide whether to break a confidence to keep someone from being hurt, discussion can reinforce what she has done well and enable time for thinking about how to respond in a similar situation.

While ethics involves being accountable for one's actions, it is rarely productive to ask young children – of whatever age – why they have acted inappropriately, however much adults wish to do so. Children only gradu-ally become able to say why they acted as they did – and when very young may not be able to. Usually, they either don't know and/or wish they hadn't; and want a way out and the chance to try again. It is more constructive to help children to articulate their thoughts about what they have done and its impact; and consider whether, and why, their actions were appropriate or what they might do differently in similar situations.

Case study – using language constructively

One day, walking along the street, I saw a boy of about 7 or 8 swinging on a small sapling, which looked likely to break. Seeing that he was observed, he looked panicked. My partner said that she was sure he didn't want to damage the tree, and he nodded vigorously in agreement; and looked relieved. Far more productive, in my view, than simply telling him off.

How adults can encourage productive talk about ethics is not straightfor-ward. First, we have a tendency, notably in the realm of morality, to talk rather than listen, to moralize and harangue rather than attend and guide. How an adult listens and her tone of voice may be more important than what she says, though remember how specific praise, for attributes and behav-iours and qualities to be encouraged, can help to thicken the narrative – and indicate how to respond in similar situations in future. Talking about ethics needs to be more like a conversation or a dialogue, with the child – or chil-dren – doing most of the talking, and the adult most of the listening – and asking questions to prompt thoughtfulness rather than a sense of inadequacy and failure. For instance, asking older children 'how do you want others to see you?' may be useful in helping children linking a sense of self to their actions. But this requires a level of (cognitive) insight and self-awareness which many children may not yet have; and runs the risk of undermining children's sense of identity if they feel 'got at' rather than supported.

Second, it is all too easy to disengage very young children by using lan-guage in too complex a way and older children too simple a manner. Such a difficulty may be true in many areas, but the abstract nature, and the dif-ficulty of talking about the complexity and individualness of feelings, seems to make this a particular hazard in the field of ethics.

Third, it is easy to discount children's views when they do not fit with what adults expect or find acceptable. Children are often, in practice, told what they are feeling or how they should feel, rather than encouraged to explore the complexity of how they are actually feeling. So, it is usually appropriate for adults to encourage children to be positive. But there are times when, like any of us, children need to be allowed to be upset or angry, without acting anti-socially, rather than for such emotions to be denied by adults or masked in the child.

Fourth, in a group, it is often hard for adults to avoid over-controlling who does most of the talking and which sorts of answer are acceptable. Mechanisms may be needed to avoid discussion being dominated by a few articulate – or at least talkative – children and to allow and encourage everyone to have their say. Very young children may find group discussion easier with definite rules, for instance with only the person holding a symbol like a toy or a stone being allowed to speak. When children are more experienced, these can be used more flexibly, allowing some interruptions and debate.

Despite these risks, what adults say can be very influential in how children develop attributes such as empathy and thoughtfulness, especially by reinforcing these, and so thickening the child's narrative and strengthening her sense of moral identity. So, language is one of the most powerful tools in how adults can help children learn to develop the attributes associated with character and ethics. Adults must seek to strengthen and support, but not rely primarily on, conscious mechanisms, especially for very young children and those for whom such mechanisms do not work very efficiently. Even more important are subtle, non-conscious mechanisms such as expectations and example.

Expectations and example

We have seen that learning is a reciprocal and social process where the expectations of, and example set by, others affect one's sense of self, particularly for young children. Chapter 5 highlighted feedback as one powerful mechanism to enhance learning, but what this actually involves for adults to encourage appropriate action and interaction, may not be always obvious.

While the most obvious type of feedback is what adults say, a more subtle and influential type comes in the form of expectations. High aspirations – hopes for, and expectations of, oneself – are vital in breaking the pattern by which children tend to be as successful, or unsuccessful, as their parents. Such aspirations are to some extent culturally transmitted. One reason why it is harder for children to learn, and teachers to teach, in a culture of low expectations is that these become self-fulfilling, not only in terms of academic attainment and behaviour, but less tangible matters such as attitudes and motivation. The expectations which adults have of children help to create, to reinforce and sometimes to undermine, children's sense of identity.

Everyone is in favour of adults having high expectations, but what this entails is more complicated than it may seem. For all children, but especially young ones, adult expectations must:

- be realistic if they are to encourage and motivate rather than discourage and disengage children;
- be broad if they are to avoid an overemphasis on academic attainment at the expense of the development of the whole child; and
- relate to attributes such as empathy and thoughtfulness if they are to discourage self-centredness and individualism.

As Good and Brophy (1990, p. 443) suggest:

> expectations tend to be self-sustaining. They affect both *perception*, by causing teachers to be alert for what they expect and less likely to notice what they do not expect, and *interpretation*, by causing teachers to interpret (perhaps to distort) what they see so that it is consistent with their expectations. Some expectations persist even though they do not coincide with the facts.

This means that adults tend to notice what we expect to and to interpret what we notice in accordance with our expectations. So, it is all too easy to give undue weight to the poor behaviour of those whom one expects to misbehave and to overlook, or make allowances for, similar behaviour in others. Even more worryingly, it means that stereotypes tend to persist although there is evidence to the contrary. Such attitudes disadvantage those already disadvantaged even further – for instance those from (some) ethnic minorities, those living troubled lives and those deemed to be of low ability. Although it is uncomfortable to do so, I remember:

- expecting Pakistani-heritage girls to be quiet and finding that they were so;
- being too 'soft' on those who thought that their difficulties meant that they had no chance of success; and
- accepting work, and behaviour, of a poor quality on the basis that a particular child could not do any better.

Therefore, adults need consciously and constantly to struggle to avoid our expectations reinforcing how such children may see themselves.

Ireson, Mortimore and Hallam (1999, p. 216) highlight a further difficulty that:

> high expectations . . . have to spring naturally from the belief and aspirations of the teacher and learner. They have to be genuine or they become counterproductive . . . Expectations are passed between teacher and learner in subtle, often undetected, ways . . . Underpinning teachers' attitudes to the capabilities of their students is their belief about intelligence . . . If . . . teachers believe that intelligence can be modified by experience, they will be more likely to pitch their expectations positively.

So, adults have to work hard (and consciously) to avoid low expectations of some children, especially those seen, and who see themselves, as of lower ability. In part, this involves trying to adopt in oneself, and encourage in children, a growth mindset where success and failure is not explained by inherent factors, such as ethnicity or ability, but related, rather, to the need for more effort, support and opportunities to try again (see Dweck, 2000, and Hart et al., 2004).

Since young children learn most by example, one of the most influential types of feedback is what adults do. Other children can provide good examples of how to conduct themselves – and when they do so may be very influential. However, adults have a particular responsibility given the nature of their relationship with the child. Personal authenticity is essential. A message from someone whom one respects rings hollow from a hypocrite. If children are to internalize attributes and dispositions to act and interact in particular ways, adults have to do more than merely to teach about these. They must 'walk the talk', so that explicit and implicit messages match. So, for example, to counter the idea that 'anything goes', adults must demonstrate that how one acts and interacts is important; and if children are to learn that internal qualities matter more than external possessions, adults must show this by their actions. If children are expected to avoid stereotyping or sarcasm, adults must do so.

Recalling Dewey's emphasis on manners as the basis of morals, children – we all – learn to be considerate by small actions such as saying please and thank you, holding doors open and noticing and responding to other people's needs and feelings. Such ordinary, everyday actions and interactions must become habitual, but based on respect for others and thoughtfulness, rather than fear or status. To encourage this, adults must model, and reinforce, such actions and attitudes. If adults want children to be honest, humble and thoughtful, they must exhibit such attributes (and be prepared to accept when they have not); and if they expect others to show respect, do so themselves.

Rogoff (1990) uses the term apprenticeship to describe an approach where the more experienced person provides an example, while those who are less experienced learn to act in similar ways primarily by watching, listening and imitating. She sees apprenticeship as involving 'guided participation'. Shulman (2004, p. 525) writes that 'the concept of apprenticeship rests on modelling after and imitating the wisdom of experience and practice . . . Apprenticeships are local, particular, situated'. In addition, apprenticeships happen over a long period of time with the craftsman treating the apprentice as if s/he is capable, though requiring further practice and guidance. These considerations make an apprenticeship model appropriate for learning and teaching procedural knowledge and practical activities, including much of what I have called real-life ethics.

Role models provide examples to which children can aspire. Chapter 3 discussed how celebrities and sportspeople often offer superficial role models of how to act. One may hold up famous people such as Mother Theresa and Nelson Mandela as examples to be copied. While often providing a powerful example of what attributes such as compassion and courage look like in practice, such an approach risks idealizing only particular types of person and the examples may be too distant for very young children. The more complex and diverse a society, the wider the range of different models of how to act and interact are needed. The less experienced the children, the closer such exemplars may need to be, so that children think 'I could do that'.

For most children, parents, teachers, other adults who care for them and other children are the most influential role models. Since ethics, especially for young children, is mostly about relatively ordinary actions and interactions, the example set must be reflected in the normal course of events through adults' small, often apparently trivial, actions. Except that they are not trivial.

So, teachers – and other adults – must model how to think, to act and to be. This may sound rather daunting. However, the teachers in Jackson et al.'s study (1993, pp. 286–7) did not use the term role model much, perhaps because it seems too 'heroic' a role. Rather than virtues such as courage, wisdom and generosity, they spoke of 'humbler virtues' such as:

- showing respect for others;
- demonstrating what it means to be intellectually absorbed;

- paying close attention to what is being said;
- being a 'good sport'; and even
- showing that it is OK to make mistakes and to be confused.

Just as children learn attributes associated with character by 'small steps', adults must demonstrate such 'humbler virtues'. Most are not obviously associated with moral education in the sense of what is right and wrong. They reflect adults attuned to children's needs and interests, responses and questions and neither over-serious, self-righteous nor too certain. How adults act and interact with children and with each other matters. Do not underestimate the effect of a smile of affirmation, or an unspoken sign of disapproval; or asking about a child's sick parent or picking up a piece of litter. These both exemplify how one should act and show that adults are not exempt from acting thoughtfully.

This chapter has presented moral education as a process occurring across the whole of life. Many different types of activity, experience and response help to develop attributes and dispositions such as the empathy and thoughtfulness fundamental to human relationships and interactions – and so to ethics. In Chapter 10, we consider how the moral dimension should, and can, be part of an approach integral to how adults think, relate and respond, and how settings operate.

10

Moving beyond Separate Programmes

Separate programmes

Arthur (2003, p. 24) laments that Britain has 'a long history of ill-conceived and ineffective efforts at character education' and that there is little in the way of empirical research or major evaluation of character education programmes in the United States or Britain.

This section considers five programmes designed to enhance young children's social, emotional and moral development, identifying strengths and limitations of each. The discussion helps explain why such programmes, however helpful in many respects, are of limited use in isolation, making the case for an approach embedded in the whole way in which institutions operate.

The SEAL (Social and Emotional Aspects of Learning) materials are intended to help children develop social and emotional skills such as empathy and cooperation and learn to avoid unkind and disruptive responses. Time is set aside, usually at least once a week, in groups, often based on circle time, where children play games and discuss their feelings, with the intention of understanding their own and other people's feelings and thinking together about strategies to respond appropriately.

SEAL has proved popular in many English primary schools, reflecting a concern about young children's social and emotional development and well-being and wish to emphasize these aspects more than in recent years. Various evaluations, both formal and otherwise, have indicated positive outcomes in terms of children's enjoyment and aspects such as empathy, self-regulation and social skills, though there is evidence of the materials being less suitable for 10- and 11-year-olds than younger children. However, as indicated in Chapter 8, Ecclestone and Hayes (2008) suggest that the emphasis on feelings in this way of working – and other similar ones – promotes an expectation that children should 'be positive', saying that they are happy, even when they are not or do not know how they feel.

The Family Links Nurturing Programme has some similarities, though a distinctive element is the joint focus on parents/carers and children, making it suitable both in schools and more widely. Games and small-group discussions (usually with parents/carers and children separate) are used to talk about feelings and responses and discuss strategies to regulate behaviour appropriately and so to avoid anti-social and aggressive behaviour. Parents/carers are:

- enabled to discuss and understand the difficulties of being parents;
- helped to understand the reasons for children's behaviour;
- encouraged to set, and stick, to clear boundaries; and
- given practical advice on how to do so.

Group leaders are trained to help parents/carers to recognize that difficulties and responses of frustration and exasperation in bringing up young children were usual; and to understand why and the need to set clear boundaries. Children are introduced to a language to talk, and think, about how they are feeling and through activities and games taught how to make friends and resolve difficulties.

Evaluations show that the Nurturing Programme has generated considerable enthusiasm, particularly where children are uncertain how to interact with each other and in families where appropriate boundaries have not been set. The impact of Family Links is strongest for very young children and their parents. However, the language used – for instance about warm and fuzzy feelings – was not universally popular and thought too 'babyish' for older children. One incident illustrates this. A 10-year-old, asked how useful the strategies were out of school, described how he had been taught when threatened to adopt a range of strategies, including TVI, short for 'That's Very Interesting'. 'Well', he said, 'do you think that saying that is going to stop a thirteen year old banging my head on the wall?' He accepted that the Nurturing Programme had many helpful features, especially in how to resolve conflict, while seeing the strategies as of limited use outside school.

Roots of Empathy is an international programme for children of elementary school age, mostly in English-speaking countries. Its mission to build caring, peaceful and civil societies through the development of empathy in children and adults. The programme involves visits every three weeks by an infant and his/her parent(s) as a basis for lessons on emotional understanding, perspective taking, caring for others and infant development. Roots of Empathy aims to decrease children's aggression and facilitate their social and emotional understanding and pro-social behaviours. The programme's website claims to have shown a significant effect in reducing levels of aggression, while raising social/emotional competence and increasing empathy. Schonert-Reichl et al. (2012), based on a substantial study with 4th–7th-grade children, indicate that teachers report significant benefits in relation to aggressive behaviour; and that children come to understand why the infant cries and to adopt prosocial behaviours, though no significant changes in empathy and perspective taking were reported.

Philosophy for Children (P4C), originally devised by Lipman, and subsequently developed by several organizations, including SAPERE (Society for the Advancement of Philosophical Enquiry and Reflection in Education) is one of many initiatives designed to develop thinking skills (see Trickey and Topping, 2004 for others). In P4C, children are taught how to create their own philosophical questions often to do with morality and choose one as the focus of a philosophical enquiry, or dialogue. P4C is based on group discussion of questions with no easy answers, emphasizing respectful listening, building on other people's views and disagreeing without confrontation. An adult facilitator supports the children in their thinking, reasoning and questioning, and how they speak and listen to each other. P4C usually takes place in separate sessions, but the skills and attributes involved can be applied in all subject areas.

Trickey and Topping's (2004) systematic review of ten evaluative studies concluded that P4C was beneficial in encouraging both talking and listening skills, though the benefits for primary age children are not specifically identified. These evaluations point to the potential of P4C across the curriculum but the difficulties of embedding this way of working in different subject areas. While using an approach based on circle time can help ensure that everyone's voice is heard, having to wait for one's turn in a big group makes it hard to build on what other people have said; and steering P4C to ensure that the group focuses on the question, but allowing children to express themselves freely, is not easy.

While the term 'values education' is used in many ways, this and the next paragraph describes Values-based Education as devised at West Kidlington Primary School, near Oxford, UK. This was characterized by Farrer (2000) as 'A Quiet Revolution' and described briefly in Eaude (2004); and adapted on a much larger scale in Australia (see Lovat and Toomey, 2007). As originally planned, Values-based Education uses a list of universal values, with twenty-two, as listed in Table 7.2 on page 113, though schools can adapt this. The whole school focuses on one value, usually for a month. Assemblies, class discussions, displays and rewards systems (both individual and collective) and as a basis for behaviour and other policies are used to help children to understand what the values entail and live accordingly. For all adults and children to (try to) model the values is essential. The list of values and discussion to show the link between these and with behaviour helps to develop a 'vocabulary of values'. Times set aside for reflection are usually part of a Values-based Education approach.

The immediate impact, often described in terms of improved behaviour and more respectful relationships between adults and children, between children and between adults, has often been considerable (see Eaude, 2004). A lack of such respect was often the rationale for schools becoming involved. One 10-year-old's comment, when he said, with great conviction, 'you need to understand that I really did not know before how to behave – and now I do', attests to the powerful impact of making such expectations explicit. The longer-term impact is harder to assess, with some indication that, as with many programmes, sustaining Values-based Education requires a lot of energy and commitment. Developing the language to help older children recognize how to deal with conflicting demands has proved difficult. Lovat and Toomey (2007) are among those who claim that Values-based Education is linked to higher levels of attainment, but the variety of ways in which such an approach operates makes it hard to sustain so general a claim.

All the programmes discussed in this section have many proponents who regard them as excellent. But their success – and that of similar ones – is often less than is claimed. This seems to be because such programmes:

1 are not sufficiently flexible, in terms of the ways of working and the language used, to be suitable for children of different ages;
2 tend to emphasize ways to control emotions and regulate behaviour, rather than how to process and respond to more difficult, and possibly conflicting, feelings;

3 are usually separate from, and sometimes marginal to, the rest of the curriculum; and seen, in practice, as less important than academic subjects, and so run the risk of being seen as an add-on;

4 inevitably, depend on how well they are used and therefore on the adults leading them.

Unsurprisingly, such programmes are more successful when adults understand and apply the underlying principles well – and more superficial when used formulaically, given the importance of sensitive, reciprocal relationships. When used well, adults model the types of conduct to be encouraged and link familiar situations to more abstract ideas, enabling children to understand what such ideas means and how these relate to their own actions. While such programmes can have a rapid, positive impact, they are often hard to sustain and develop, either because they lose momentum after a time, or the initial messages become stale or over-simple as children grow older and encounter more complex issues. So, any programme, or approach, has to, and be seen to, refer to a wide range of situations and requires regular refreshing to retain its vitality. This emphasizes the need for any approach to character education to be embedded throughout the whole life of the setting.

Balancing conflicting priorities

When a headteacher was discussing with me the ideas in this book, she asked 'didn't I think that all children should be literate and numerate?' My answer was that of course I did, but this was not all that I wanted or that literacy and mathematics were the only areas I regarded as basic. In thinking how to educate children, one must return to aims, what one hopes to achieve, and this must, in my view, particularly for young children, entail a broad sense of well-being. And as highlighted in Chapter 4, resolving dilemmas between conflicting priorities is inherent in working with children, both in formal settings and otherwise.

Moral educators – whatever their role – are never concerned only with morality and ethics and must be aware of, and try to find a path through the demanding terrain discussed in Chapters 3 and 4, avoiding the pitfalls highlighted in Chapter 1. Such a path involves balancing different considerations; and therefore making judgements, both long term and immediate, taking account of the demands of expectations and policies and the realities of day-to-day life.

Before exploring some practical implications, let me amplify two general points. The first is that Chapters 3 and 4 considered how the society in which children grow up and the current educational climate emphasize pace, as if life were a race to be run, often at a breathless speed, rather than a journey to be savoured. In a world where many children do not receive much adult attention and boundaries are often unclear, they need space, time and guidance, to question, experiment, imagine and test out boundaries, if they are to internalize the reasons for their actions, rather than just comply.

Chapter 8 cautioned against misusing the power inherent in working with young children. Character education is more a question of influencing and guiding than of telling or forcing. In thinking how to exercise such influence, an analogy with sport or cooking may help. It is not enough to give children a ball and expect them to learn to be good footballers on their own, but neither is it appropriate to introduce them to the intricacies of the off-side rule too soon. One does not just provide the ingredients and the recipe and expect children to bake a cake on their own. Young players and cooks have to be guided and introduced gradually to the complexities, but without getting into bad habits.

The same applies, even more, in the realm of ethics. Few would argue that children should not at times be reprimanded or reward or sanction (of some sort) used to reinforce or discourage particular types of behaviour. However, in the long term, care, nurture and example are more likely to encourage attributes such as empathy and generosity, and the disposition and motivation to manifest these even when the going gets tough.

From this, a second point follows, that there is no one way to 'do' moral education, in either its broader or narrower sense. The research on expertise (see Eaude, 2012) indicates that expertise, in whatever field, is prototypical, situated and largely tacit. In other words:

- there are many different ways of manifesting expertise;
- how to do so depends on the context; and
- it is hard to put one's finger on exactly how those with a high level of expertise work.

As Haydon (2004, p. 116) suggests, sustaining the ethical environment 'does not indicate a specific model for teachers to follow . . . (but) does suggest a particular way of looking at the responsibility of teachers in the area of values education'. Seeing character, or indeed personal, social, emotional or moral, education as a separate subject or discrete part of education is at best limiting. Developing the whole child requires an approach which permeates, as far as possible, the whole range of children's experience and influences their response and motivation at a deep level.

One tricky question is to what extent an emphasis on care and empathy may conflict with one on academic standards and attainment. While the moral dimension should be an integral part of any learning environment, there are many other dimensions – among them academic, social and physical – and adults have other priorities. The pressure for measurable outcomes, even with very young children, is much stronger than twenty years ago and seems unlikely to diminish. Indeed it may increase further. However, Hattie (2009, pp. 126–8) suggests that non-cognitive variables such as teacher expectations and teacher–student relationships have a stronger correlation with academic outcomes than cognitive ones such as teachers' subject knowledge. And Alexander (2010) cites a wide range of research indicating that a broad curriculum is not inimical to high standards of attainment in the long term but the best way to achieve them; quite apart from being more inclusive and addressing the needs of the whole child. A curriculum narrowly focused on 'the basics' runs counter to how young children learn best. Moreover, it is likely to be disengaging, and even damaging, for those whose experience outside school means that such a curriculum fails to engage their interest or who find such learning difficult.

You may think an emphasis on care appropriate with very young children, but less so for those who are 10 or 11 years old. Most traditions of bringing up, and teaching, very young children recognize the importance of care and nurture, but increasingly emphasize challenge and academic attainment for older children. But we all – some more than others – require care and nurture at times if we are to thrive; and need both to be cared-for and to care-for other people and the natural world, if we are to become more empathetic and compassionate. These needs continue for longer than we tend to recognize; and caring-for-others seems to be particularly beneficial, though difficult, for those unused to being cared-for. The ethic of care may have to be expressed in different, more sophisticated, ways with older children, but the need to be cared-for, and to care-for, does not disappear.

There is a danger that the harder teachers strive for immediate results, the less they expect, and enable, children to develop mastery-oriented qualities such as a belief in their own capability and persistence in the face of difficulties. So, it is worth considering Noddings' (1991, p. 161) words that:

> schools should become places in which teachers and students live together, talk to each other, reason together, take delight in each others' company. Like good parents, teachers should be concerned first and foremost with the kind of people their charges are becoming. My guess is that when schools focus on what really matters in life, the cognitive ends we are now striving towards in such painful and artificial ways will be met as natural culminations of the means we have widely chosen.

Creating an appropriate environment which addresses the multiple aims of education entails finding an appropriate balance between:

- pace and space;
- care and challenge;
- structure and freedom;
- prohibition and guidance.

Children's needs may vary and the circumstances of their lives change, but learning how to act and interact appropriately is an active process requiring a sense of agency and engagement. While adults must remain in control, they must not over-control and have to learn to live with sometimes uncomfortable tensions between prescribing and allowing, accepting and challenging, simplifying and complicating.

Balancing these conflicting priorities entails adults making judgements based on their relationships with, and knowledge of, the children, their families and other significant adults and the circumstances of children's lives. Without being attuned to these and how children are feeling, and personal authenticity – setting a good example and 'walking the talk' – it is hard to see how adults can create an inclusive, nurturing environment.

While judgement is essential, some general principles on how adults should work with young children in developing character may be helpful. Opposite is a list of twelve principles, summarizing key points of the last three chapters.

Twelve principles to consider in character education with young children

1 Seek to develop broad learning attributes rather than only 'moral' ones.
2 Weave an ethical dimension into everything rather than seeing ethics as separate.
3 Create and sustain an environment where everyone has a sense of agency and belonging.
4 Welcome and celebrate diversity of belief and background.
5 Look to create space(s) and time(s) for reflection and discussion.
6 Listen and watch to be attuned to how children are feeling and acting.
7 Question and guide more than tell and prescribe.
8 Be confident and predictable, but not too certain or inflexible.
9 Reinforce 'small steps' and what children should (rather than shouldn't) do.
10 Expect children to conduct themselves thoughtfully and do so yourself.
11 Demonstrate the 'humbler virtues' rather than thinking you have to be perfect.
12 Work collaboratively with other adults significant in children's lives.

How individual adults – parents, teachers and others – operate matters, but moral education is not just an individual concern. The next two sections consider the challenges of working with others and the benefit of a collective approach.

Working in partnership

Children's patterns of response are strongly influenced well before they reach formal settings. Early experience, in the home and local community, provides a foundation, for better or worse, of how children regulate their behaviour and responses. Children spend much longer out of, than in, school, with these experiences exerting a considerable, and ongoing, influence on their attitudes and beliefs.

Moral education is not just a matter for family members, or those in formal settings, or voluntary groups, but occurs throughout life; and is ideally a collaborative partnership, where children receive similar and complementary messages from the various adults in their lives. Whatever one's role, this involves working with other adults significant in the child's life, recognizing that all have different roles and may bring different assumptions and beliefs. We have seen that children, and families, have varying beliefs and expectations. While most obviously related to ethnicity and religion, such differences may relate to culture in the sense of social class or upbringing. The media present a range of powerful messages about how one should act. There is at best a fragile consensus on how children should act and interact.

Ideally, this partnership involves parents/carers and all those who work in different settings outside the home. Those who teach young children have a strong tradition of working with parents/carers to help children to settle in an unfamiliar environment, with new, more complex challenges. However, this is not always so; and often not easy.

In Chapter 1, I suggested that blaming others is a pitfall to avoid. Arthur (2010, p. 36) may be correct when he writes, 'the school cannot hope to substitute for the family, but it sometimes has to compensate for the failure of the family in the formation of character'. But sometimes families and voluntary groups may have to compensate for the school. Schools have a vital role in affirming the 'moral order', showing that how one acts and interacts matters and operating in ways which include and support all children, especially the least resilient. But schools have no monopoly of moral education and can easily overlook the moral dimension in a culture of performativity and competition.

Since many of the most significant aspects of the moral life of schools – and other settings – are implicit in adults' ways of working and expectations, people who do not understand and share these are at a disadvantage unless these are made explicit – and explained. Without this, there is a danger that many children and their families will *de facto* be excluded.

Most adults are keen to see children adopt broadly similar beliefs, values and virtues to their own. For most parents/carers, this is less problematic than for those adults who have to address the needs of a large, diverse group. Teachers, especially, easily find themselves in the horns of a dilemma, wishing to assert that some ways of acting and interacting are appropriate and others not, while recognizing that some families quite legitimately have varying beliefs and values. But, as Bruner (1990, p. 30) writes, 'open-mindedness is the keystone of what we call a democratic culture', continuing that this implies 'a willingness to construe knowledge and values from multiple perspectives, without loss of commitment to one's own values'. In a time of change, 'confident uncertainty' – an ability to tolerate ambiguity, leaving space for uncertainty and the unknown, being open to different views without losing one's confidence about what one believes in – or what Hill (1981) calls 'committed impartiality' – becomes particularly important for those working in schools.

Chapter 8 emphasized the importance of adult expectations in helping to shape character and identity. The success of any approach to moral education involves attending to the relationships between, and the mutual expectations of, all adults and children in a setting. So, while, in a school, the headteacher has to take a lead in setting a good example, this responsibility must be shared, as far as possible, by all adults – whatever their role. Support staff may often be particularly well-placed in providing space for children to explore their feelings and responses, because they often work in small groups. In contrast, teachers are often expected to concentrate more on 'academic' learning and are usually working with a whole class.

Office staff are often the first point of contact and those who relate particularly to children who are late or unwell and parents/carers; and so are very important in welcoming newcomers and dealing with those who are worried. How site managers respond to children when they have lost a ball or a coat their help affects how children learn to conduct themselves. Those supervising at lunchtimes have a role in helping children to learn how to act and interact, although often they have the least training for the least structured time during the day; and even usually well-behaved children are ruder towards them than they would dream of being with other adults. While it is more difficult for schools to ensure that visitors espouse the school's values and ways of working, it is helpful to make them aware of the school's expectations; and important that regular visitors, such as those who lead assemblies or take after-school clubs, recognize and abide by these.

Let us think about the implications when expectations from home and those at school clash. If teachers are to uphold the 'moral order', they must set boundaries that some actions are not acceptable, even if they are outside school. Some, like hurting other children deliberately, must be regarded as non-negotiable; and learning to cooperate with others is one central aspect of the socializing aspect of school.

The situation is far from straightforward on issues such as 'hitting back' or racist comments, if such behaviours are encouraged by a parent. While responding to such situations can be difficult, most teachers say something on the lines of 'we sort out problems in a different way at school', usually with an appeal to school rules and an explanation of why. If the child is not to be confused or torn between conflicting loyalties, it helps if parents/carers understand and, where possible, support this, and if disagreements are discussed between adults, rather than in the presence of the children. In practice, most parents/carers will recognize (and welcome) that the school has expectations of caring and thoughtful conduct. Even those parents/carers who disagree with these and want their child to learn to stand up for themselves are likely to agree, at least in principle, not to undermine the school's approach. For teachers and parents/carers at least to recognize what each other wants, even if not agree on the means to achieve this, may help. But asserting the moral order means that ultimately some issues are non-negotiable.

The situation is more complex for legitimate areas of difference, described in Chapter 7 as secondary values, and often related to cultural and religious beliefs and norms. There is a danger of schools' expectations conflicting with practices and beliefs which matter profoundly for some families or cultures, in areas such as diet, clothing and sex education. In some systems, these may be largely a matter for schools to decide, whereas in others, the constitution or the law may determine the parameters more closely.

Some parents may see moral education as their province, with the teachers' role mainly academic. So, such differences call for considerable sensitivity. For example, in England, while most schools would be prepared to provide vegetarian meals, there may be more reticence about providing *halal* or *kosher* food – and not just because of questions of practicability or cost. Schools may be prepared to allow for tracksuits and trousers for girls and provide single-sex changing, especially as children approach puberty; but less sure about wearing headscarfs. However, inclusivity would seem to require that schools try to be accommodating, where possible, on such issues. Awareness of how important these are to some families and a commitment to discussion, without compromising the school's values, usually means that a way of working together can be found. Where this is not possible, schools should be prepared at the least to justify their decisions.

Adults can influence, but never in the long term control, what children become. It may help to see the task of all adults as foundational, in that they have a responsibility to encourage widely agreed ways of acting and interacting – such as showing respect and acting in the interests of the group. Some, especially those whose role is more explicitly moral or religious, may wish to add a superstructure of beliefs and ways of understanding and exemplifying these. So, I suggest that schools and other settings should:

- assert that how children (and adults) act and interact matters and set out expectations for what these entail for everyone within that setting; but
- restrict these to areas of widely agreed norms of conduct, leaving scope for matters of individual or group preference.

There is likely to be a greater commonality on attributes to be developed than on specific rules to be followed. This underlies my belief that virtue ethics provides a more promising and flexible approach than duty ethics in a world of diverse beliefs.

Towards a virtue ethics approach

This book has suggested that many current assumptions should be challenged, including:

- social and cultural ones about success and happiness; and
- educational ones about the aims of education and ways to achieve these.

Individuals do not work alone, in a bubble. Any environment operates within, and is affected by, the environment outside. An individual can make a difference, but this is far easier where everyone adopts a similar approach and mutual expectations are articulated and supported throughout the life of the institution – whether a school or a voluntary group. So, moral education requires institutional, as well as personal, authenticity. This section suggests what this entails and why virtue ethics provides an appropriate and flexible way of influencing children for good and enabling adults to do so.

As Williams (2000, p. 92) puts it:

moral education is neither the imparting of rules in a vacuum nor the discussion of how young people (think they) decide issues, but is bound up with the roles and responsibilities actually and actively learned in the corporate life of an institution . . . It is no use at all to pontificate about the need for 'values' to be communicated if the entire style and pace of an institution allow no room for understanding learning in their diversity, or if the institution moves more and more towards a monochrome version of what learning is ('training'); if the institution sees its task as the – increasingly anxious and hurried – job of passing on information and measurable skills at the expense of reflection on the character of its common life as educative.

So, values must be related to, and influence, everyday life and decisions and permeate every aspect of how schools and other settings operate; and one should be wary of any approach which sees education in narrow, instrumental terms. A system which encourages individualism, competitiveness and pace, and leaves little room for collective action, cooperation and space for reflection, will create losers as well as winners.

Pring (2007, p. 123) reinforces this view, writing:

> the school . . . is essentially a moral *community*, if that is what it is, in which, through participation, the young person grows as a moral person, learns how to interact fruitfully with other people, benefits from the different ways of understanding experience, learns how to work cooperatively with others for the good of the whole, builds up a common experience, welcomes through work and play the close association with others, and is continuous with the wider community outside the school.

Schools have an important role in providing an inclusive environment for all children to experience, and discuss, a good life characterized by mutual respect. This matters particularly for those who do not experience a similar environment elsewhere, for whatever reason. However, creating and sustaining a learning environment with space and time for exploring and developing a sense of identity is hard in the current policy context with its insistence on pace, coverage and conformity, and the strong pressure for measurable outcomes. Many current approaches and assumptions highlighted in Chapter 4 give messages which, through the hidden curriculum, discourage children from exploring, and reflecting on, how they should act and interact, rather than just complying with adults' expectations in terms of behaviour.

Chapter 1 set out McLaughlin and Halstead's (1999) description of two main strands of moral education, though any approach may adopt aspects of each. I have argued against reliance on a set of universal values and discrete programmes of moral education; suggesting, rather, that the attributes associated with ethics are internalized more through the hidden curriculum and modelling, repetition and habit than direct instruction and conscious reasoning. The moral dimension should run through every aspect of provision. In particular, children from an early age must learn to exercise judgement about the most appropriate course of action, in context, supported, where necessary, by more experienced others. An approach relying primarily on conscious and rational processes is likely to be superficial, unless underpinned by cultivating the more deeply rooted traits associated with character.

In some ways, moral education is very complex, but paradoxically simpler than it may seem. We have seen that there is no 'quick-fix', but that a gradual, 'drip-drip', approach is required, with adults aware of the moral dimension in all that they do and concentrating mostly on everyday actions and inter-actions and processes. Content and language matter and programmes and instruction may be valuable, but example and relationships matter more. There is no one template or manual to follow. While any approach must take account of considerations such as the age of the children and the type of setting, an apprenticeship model and virtue ethics provides a flexible frame-work on which a suitable approach can be based.

Chapter 2 described briefly what virtue ethics entails. Carr (2007, p. 373) writes that 'the compelling appeal of virtue ethics is that it shows precisely how the often distinguished and separated cognitive, affective, social and motivational aspects of moral life may be coherently re-connected'. Virtue ethics does not rely primarily on reasoning, but sees morality as based on the sort of person one is, and becomes. In Carr's (ibid.) words:

> although Aristotle is keen to press the point that morality is grounded in practice – a point recognised in his famous analogy between the cultivation of virtues and the acquisition of skills – he equally clearly takes such character training to be necessary but not sufficient for virtue. Indeed, he is equally emphatic that full acquisition of the moral virtues of courage, temperance and justice requires the principled reflection of practical wisdom.

So, while of course children – we all – must learn to reflect on, and reason about, more specifically moral questions, and act accordingly, this requires a foundation rooted in the internal qualities associated with character.

One strength of virtue ethics when working with young children in a diverse world is that it highlights specific attributes to be encouraged, while leaving open what these are and exactly how, and to what extent, they should be manifested. Virtue ethics provides the basis of a language to guide conduct and exemplify abstract ideas which is sufficiently flexible for use in many different contexts, both religious and secular. Whether the actual language used with children is that of values or virtues matters less than an emphasis on exhibiting such attributes and learning to balance conflicting demands in finding the most appropriate course of action. Distinguishing between primary and secondary virtues may help, particularly with older children, to differentiate those which are broadly shared from those more culturally determined, recognizing both similarity and difference. So, virtue ethics offers a non-prescriptive, nuanced approach suitable for a diverse world.

A second strength is that virtue ethics provides scope for children increasingly to develop an enhanced understanding, and practice, of ethics. While it may be necessary to give simple messages to very young children or those finding it hard to regulate their emotional responses, children – we all – have to learn to make judgements about how to act appropriately in a particular context. A vocabulary of ethics helps to provide a way of thinking about what this entails – and virtue ethics offers a sophisticated, unpreachy language to do so at different levels. But more fundamental is cultivating attributes such as care, empathy and compassion, and for these to be exemplified and made habitual and so embedded, as far as possible, throughout children's lives.

A third strength is that virtue ethics is easily integrated into an approach based on learning attributes and qualities, such as that proposed by Claxton (2002) or those based on Dweck's (2000) ideas; and therefore avoids the moral being seen as separate from other dimensions of education and among teachers, especially, a sense of initiative fatigue.

This chapter has started to draw together different threads of the argument, indicating that, while there is no one way to 'do' moral education, no manual or programme to be followed, the moral dimension should run through the whole life of institutions; and that practising personal and institutional authenticity is more likely to influence children for good than prescribing a code of rules or using specific programmes.

11

Gathering the Threads

The introduction described this book as like a tapestry or a collage, with the final picture only emerging gradually. The first four chapters explored the context in which children grow up and moral educators work. The next three considered how young children learn, focusing on how early experience affects the development of identity and character and how emotion can disable conscious learning mechanisms. The third part discussed how adults can best support children's moral development, emphasizing environments and expectations, relationships and example and suggesting that an approach based on virtue ethics is appropriate for a world of diversity and change.

This chapter pulls together these different threads, trying to summarize the implications in relation to ethics, children, adults and, briefly, policy. I highlight what I see as distinctive about the picture created, though you will, inevitably, draw out the elements most relevant to your own context.

Implications for ethics

The picture of ethics I have painted is a broad one, based on actions more than intentions, on relationships more than rationality, on context more than rules, suggesting that:

- most actions have both technical and ethical dimensions;
- the boundary between these is less clear than is usually assumed; and
- morality and ethics must not be compartmentalized into a separate part of one's life.

This is not to say that intentions, rationality and rules do not matter – they do – but that the focus of moral education should be on actions, relationships and context – and therefore on developing judgement and intrinsic motivation. Moreover, moral education does not just happen at home or school, but throughout life.

The surrounding culture affects us all, but children particularly strongly. The current culture, based on materialism, trivialization and celebrity encourages self-interest, individualism and narcissism and has a profound effect in the models of success and aspiration provided. The result is confusion rather than moral decline. So adults should not succumb to moral panic, but seek to equip children to negotiate a path through this uncertain terrain. In challenging many current assumptions about the source of happiness and success, I have argued that children must be helped to recognize that many of these are open to question and that internal, intangible factors matter more than external, tangible ones.

I have tried to outline an adaptable approach which can act as the foundation for those with different bases of ethics – those of autonomy, community and divinity – without adopting the attractive, but illusory, view of values as universal. Universalism, however appealing it may seem, does not reflect the context-related and culturally defined nature of ethics. The lack of consensus about which virtues and values one should espouse is increasingly obvious in a diverse and globalized world.

My approach is, broadly, a communitarian one, based on an ethic of care and relationships, rather than one based on individualism and reasoning. While duty ethics, based on the application of rules, provides a clear, and familiar, basis for moral education, I have suggested that this is fragile; and more controversially, that, while religion can provide for some people a sound basis of ethics, this risks being fragile if based on rules rather than attributes. Moreover, a view of morality based on religious belief is inappropriate outside the context of faith communities. While for children to be happy is desirable, making the search for happiness the basis of ethics is dangerous in a world where so many attractive, but illusory, routes to a good life are on offer. Similarly, while children's rights must be taken seriously, the discourse of rights risks becoming too individualistic unless balanced by a corresponding emphasis on responsibilities towards others.

In line with Gilligan's and Noddings' work, relationships, empathy and care – both being cared-for and caring-for others – should be at the heart of both ethics and moral education. Choices are more likely to be appropriate when one considers the possible consequences for other people than when relying on abstract principles and reasoning. The ethic of care highlights essential elements of a broad sense of well-being, achieved more through relationships, altruism and service to others than consumption and external, superficial markers of identity.

There is no point at which children become suddenly moral beings. One should not assume that adults act more ethically than children and should be wary of traditions, such as that associated with Kohlberg, which see moral development as a linear, upward, one-way journey. We are all capable of change for the worse as well as for the better and need the support of others.

The prime task is to enable children to realize that how they act and interact matters, rather than 'anything goes'. Ethics is about actions in real-life situations rather than abstract moral dilemmas and based on intrinsic motivation rather than the promise of reward or the fear of punishment. Recognizing that even very young children have some understanding of concepts such as fairness and compassion, the main challenge for moral educators is how to enable and encourage children to apply these in their actions.

For young children, especially, this involves learning to act and interact appropriately in everyday situations and for the right reasons – what Dewey called minor morals. This does not downplay the importance of language to help link abstract ideas to specific actions and inform judgement of how to act and interact appropriately in specific contexts. But it does emphasize that moral education is a practical activity, involving an interplay of non-conscious and conscious processes. The knowledge required is mainly procedural and habitual rather than propositional and one-off. A sense of how to respond in certain types of situation is developed by experience and supported by feedback to reinforce particular attributes associated with character, some general, some more specific to ethics, which help shape one's identity. So, this view of ethics and moral education challenges many of the assumptions underlying current approaches to schooling.

How individuals act in specific situations matters, but even more important in the long term are the underlying beliefs, attributes and attitudes which prompt their behaviour. So, I have argued for an approach based on character and virtue ethics, which articulates what these are. Reclaiming the idea of primary and secondary virtues has been proposed as a solution to the problem of a lack of consensus about how one should act and interact, without accepting that 'anything goes'.

Implications for children

For adults to understand how young children learn is necessary to realize how they learn to act and interact appropriately. The research indicates how different learning mechanisms operate. So, for instance:

- watching, and then acting in a similar way, provides a powerful means of learning;
- habituation embeds, and makes automatic, particular behaviours;
- analogy helps to illustrate similarities and differences; and
- executive function enables one to regulate one's behaviour.

These learning mechanisms do not operate separately and emotion and cognition are more closely linked than is usually recognized.

The discussion of internal working models resulting from attachment and primary socialization emphasizes that:

- early experience affects patterns of responses profoundly;
- engagement and agency are vital in meaning-making; and
- learning is a reciprocal and a mainly social process.

Since intense emotion easily interferes with conscious processes, anxiety, especially, must be contained. For young children and those with the least security and confidence, predictable, trusting relationships are essential to provide safety, sustain engagement and enable imagination and exploration. This is not to argue that conscious processes and language are unimportant, but that other processes are more fundamental.

The research emphasizes the brain's plasticity, so that it is constantly shaped and reshaped, during early childhood and adolescence and, to some extent, subsequently. So while early experience is very influential in how one responds in later life, patterns of behaviour are not set in stone. Identity and character can change, but remain fairly constant long-term influences on behaviour. While rooted in early experience, identity is fluid and constantly shifting. One's sense of agency and identity is influenced, for good or ill, by the perceptions of others. Developing a robust identity requires a sense of agency, a mindset that one is capable of change and the imagination to understand how other people feel and the impact of people's actions – including one's own on others. But such agency is easily undermined when children's existing identity, culture and 'funds of knowledge' – prior and existing experiences, interests and beliefs – are ignored or regarded as of little or no value.

Given the prevalence of approaches to behaviour management based on choice and consequence, one must recognize that young children's ability to regulate their behaviour develops only slowly, requiring both practice and support. The disposition not to act in self-interested ways is easily undermined by factors such as fear and peer pressure. So, ethics does not just involve propositional knowledge, but the motivation and disposition to act in caring and compassionate ways, in particular situations where principles clash and where one cannot be sure, for instance, about how brave or how respectful to be. This requires exercising judgement from an early age about what is appropriate – what I called the Goldilocks approach, not too much, not too little, consistent with Aristotle's view of virtue.

Representing experience kinaesthetically and visually helps to embed knowledge more deeply than doing so symbolically, especially through language. Young children learn by observing, practicing and, above all, living a good life, mostly in everyday situations, rather than reasoning about moral dilemmas. Since much of the language of ethics is abstract and unfamiliar, a vocabulary of ethics helps to connect such ideas to the specific realities of everyday life. While terms such as character, values and virtue can all be problematic, they help to illustrate abstract ideas, providing the basis of such a vocabulary. Like any language, this must be capable of increasingly sophisticated use.

Enabling children to flourish in a world of diversity and change requires many things which young children find difficult. While bonding with, and belonging to, groups consisting of those who are similar is essential, in a diverse world we all must learn also to bridge with those who are different. Similarly, while predictability is important, children must gradually learn to cope with what is unexpected and unpredictable.

The promise of reward and the fear of punishment are fragile bases for ethics in the long term. While non-negotiable rules have a place, especially for young children and those who find self-regulation difficult, more general maxims encourage children to consider the impact on other people and so to make more thoughtful decisions.

Implications for adults

The nature of ethics means that all adults – parents/carers, teachers and others – have a role in helping children to recognize that how they act and interact matters and enabling them find ways to cope through the confusing world which they encounter. But one must avoid, as far as possible, the pitfalls identified, particularly indoctrination and hypocrisy, and being too didactic or too certain. Those working with young children should be sensitive to the unequal power in the child–adult relationship and wary of how they can easily misuse the power they have and of a sense of moral superiority; and so should be prepared to attend to, and learn from, children.

Moral education involves influencing children for good, both in helping them to act and interact appropriately; and having a profound and long-term effect. Such a view emphasizes the role of character and is a matter for all adults with whom the child comes into contact. Some, notably parents/carers and teachers, have distinctive roles but moral education is a far more subtle task than 'telling children what is right and wrong'. Usually even very young children 'know' how they should act, but find it hard to do so. Rather, adults need to shape identities without being too prescriptive, developing the attributes, dispositions and intrinsic motivation to act and interact appropriately in a world of uncertainty. This involves modelling how to act and interact, 'walking the talk', and helping children maintain a sense of agency and a growth mindset, the sense that they are (at least to some extent) in control of how they conduct themselves, so that children internalize a framework to guide their actions when having to act autonomously.

In setting out a constructivist approach, I have argued that the task of moral educators is one of supporting children to maintain and develop their sense of agency and identity – both individual and collective – and intrinsic motivation. Adults have to balance conflicting priorities, for instance to:

- equip as well as protect;
- care as well as challenge; and
- guide rather than prescribe.

and so must exercise judgement, rather than follow a script, if learning is to be reciprocal and deep-rooted.

An inclusive learning environment provides hospitable space and maintains the moral order in which all children learn to belong and where adults take account of children's prior experience and funds of knowledge. Hospitable space depends on invitation rather than coercion, where anxiety is contained, enabling those within it to explore, and discuss, how to act and interact without the emotional cost involved in doing so and getting it wrong. This is hard to create in a culture obsessed with grading, pace and measurable outcomes. An ethic of care requires adults to care for children and encourage them to care for, and empathize with, others. The moral order, encouraging appropriate action and challenging unkindness and discrimination, matters particularly for those who do not experience such an environment in other parts of their lives.

Adults must offer predictability rather than complete consistency if they are to take account of different children's responses and prior experience and (often-difficult) lives. An emphasis on internal qualities is more long term than one based on rules and external rewards. However, if such an approach is to avoid being superficial and disengaging, varying ways of presenting what these qualities entail are needed. While rules may be necessary, maxims are more helpful in encouraging judgement. Routines help to create a sense of belonging but must not become constraining.

To be inclusive an environment must offer a breadth of opportunities and encouragement to work with others, to bridge as well as to bond, to reflect on one's actions and interactions. I have argued against the view that moral or character education should be a subject or a discrete part of the curriculum. An ethical dimension or component runs through every aspect of children's and adults' lives and the life of an institution. Activities such as play and stories which help to develop empathy and imagination in noncoercive ways are likely to be valuable. How learning processes take place and are supported matters more than the activities or content. While children and adults must learn, and develop, a vocabulary of ethics, my emphasis has been on children talking and thinking together rather than just listening to adults; and feedback as a two-way process, from adult to child and vice versa.

Giving feedback enables adults to 'thicken the narrative', children's sense of moral identity, by reinforcing positive conduct without resorting to facile praise. While spoken feedback helps to do this, even more important is that given more subtly by example and expectations. Explicit expectations must be achievable and broad as well as high; and long as well as short term. Implicit expectations include the belief in a growth mindset, that everyone is capable of change, whatever their prior experience. This is perhaps the hardest aspect of all in a school system which privileges a narrow view of success and individual competition.

Receiving feedback from children is essential if adults are to meet the needs of particular individuals and groups. This requires attunement to their needs, helping to explain why the adult/child relationship is so important; but adults need also to be willing to explain their actions and the humility to accept that, like everyone else, one does not always live up to one's ideals, but that this should not stop one from trying to do so.

While the task may seem rather daunting, I have suggested an emphasis on care, on social and emotional learning and on 'humbler virtues'. This tends to come naturally to adults working with very young children, though less so with older children in a climate of anxiety with a focus on attainment in a narrow range of subject areas. However, such an approach need not compromise the search for high scores in tests; and will provide the basis for a broader view of success than one based on such results.

Any approach at institutional level must be holistic and authentic, where the values espoused are lived and where, as far as possible, these permeate the whole life of the institution. So, I have suggested an approach broadly based on an apprenticeship model of learning and virtue ethics. An apprenticeship model takes account of how young children learn by example, over time, and avoids the pitfalls of hypocrisy and moralizing. Two particular strengths of virtue ethics are that it encourages discernment of context to establish how much one should manifest a particular quality and that it is flexible enough to be applicable, with some adaptation, to all settings, both secular and religious. This makes it possible to bring together the broader sense of moral education where a moral dimension runs through every aspect and the narrower sense of enabling children to live a good life – one where children thrive and can relate appropriately to a wide range of other people.

Implications for policy

This book is not about policy, but the implication of the argument is that many aspects of educational policy described in Chapter 4, however well-intentioned, are misguided, especially for young children. The emphasis on performativity and compliance has led to a narrowing of the curriculum and *de facto* a sidelining of the moral dimension of education. Manualization is particularly inappropriate in the field of ethics because adults must respond to children's different behaviours and ideas in order to understand and help shape their beliefs. So, more time and resource must be invested in helping teachers – and other adults – understand how the needs of the whole child are interlinked. Doing this, and changing how the formal curriculum is formulated and schools are inspected, will help to create more trust in the judgement of teachers and provide a sounder basis for such trust.

This book started by referring to the nursery headteacher who objected strongly to my question about whether a good learning environment would have a moral element, on the grounds that it was not for her to tell children what is right or wrong. It ends with the thought that maybe she would approve of what I have described as moral education, even if she may not have recognized it as such.

Bibliography

Alexander, R. (1995) *Versions of Primary Education*. London: Routledge.

Alexander, R. (2000) *Culture and Pedagogy: International Comparisons in Primary Education*. Oxford: Blackwell.

Alexander, R. (ed.) (2010) *Children, Their World, Their Education – Final Report and Recommendations of the Cambridge Primary Review*. Abingdon: Routledge.

Anderson, C. A., A. Shibuya, N. Ihori, E. L. Swing, B. J. Bushman, A. Sakamoto, H. R. Rothstein and M. Saleem (2010) 'Violent Video Game Effects on Aggression, Empathy, and Prosocial Behavior in Eastern and Western Countries: A Meta-Analytic Review', *Psychological Bulletin 136* (2): 151–73.

Anning, A. (1997) *The First Years At School*. Buckingham: Open University Press.

Arendt, H. (1970) *Men in Dark Times*. London: Cape.

Argyris, C. and D. A. Schon (1974) *Theory in Practice: Increasing Professional Effectiveness*. New York: Jossey Bass.

Aristotle (1998) *Nicomachean Ethics*. Oxford: Oxford University Press.

Arthur, J. (2003) *Education with Character: The Moral Economy of Schooling*. London: RoutledgeFalmer.

Arthur, J. (2010) *Of Good Character: Exploration of Virtues and Values in 3–25 Year-Olds*. Exeter: Imprint Academic.

Baldwin, J. (1991) *Nobody Knows My Name*. Harmondsworth: Penguin.

Ball, S. J. (2003) 'The Teacher's Soul and the Terrors of Performativity', *Journal of Education Policy 18* (2): 215–28.

Baron-Cohen, S. (2011) *Zero Degrees of Empathy: A New Theory of Human Cruelty*. London: Allen Lane.

Berger, P. and T. Luckmann (1967) *The Social Construction of Reality*. London: Allen Lane.

Berlak, A. and H. Berlak (1987) *Dilemmas of Schooling – Teaching and Social Change*. London: Methuen.

Blakemore, S.-J. and U. Frith (2005) *The Learning Brain: Lessons for Education*. Oxford: Blackwell.

Bloom, P. (2013) *Just Babies – The Origins of Good and Evil*. London: The Bodley Head.

Bowlby, J. (1965) *Child Care and the Growth of Love*. London: Penguin.

Brantlinger, E. (2003) *Dividing Classes: How the Middle Class Negotiates and Rationalizes School Advantage.* London: RoutledgeFalmer.

Bruner, J. (1990) *Acts of Meaning.* Cambridge, MA: Harvard University Press.

Bruner, J. (1996) *The Culture of Education.* Cambridge, MA: Harvard University Press.

Bruner, J. (2006) *In Search of Pedagogy (Volume 11).* Abingdon: Routledge.

Carr, D. (2003) 'Character and Moral Choice in the Cultivation of Virtue', *Philosophy 78*: 219–32.

Carr, D. (2007) 'Character in Teaching', *British Journal of Educational Studies 55* (4): 369–89.

CBI (Confederation of British Industry) (2012) *First Steps- a New Approach for Our Schools.* Available at: www.cbi.org.uk.

Clark, A. (2006) 'Language, Embodiment, and the Cognitive Niche', *Trends in Cognitive Sciences 10* (8): 370–4.

Claxton, G. (1997) *Hare Brain, Tortoise Mind: Why Intelligence Increases When You Think Less.* London: Fourth Estate.

Claxton, G. (2002) *Building Learning Power.* Bristol: TLO Ltd.

Claxton, G. and Carr, M. (2004) 'A Framework for Teaching Learning: The Dynamics of Disposition', *Early Years 24* (1): 87–97.

Claxton, G. (2005) *An Intelligent Look at Emotional Intelligence.* London: Association of Teachers and Lecturers.

Claxton, G. (2007) 'Expanding Young Children's Capacity to Learn', *British Journal of Educational Studies 55* (2): 115–34.

Coles, R. (1997) *The Moral Intelligence of Children.* London: Bloomsbury.

Cooling, T. (2010) *Doing God in Education.* London: Theos.

Cupitt, D. (1995) *What Is a Story?* London: SCM.

Cunningham, H. (2006) *The Invention of Childhood.* London: BBC Books.

Deakin Crick, R. and C. Goldspink (2014) 'Learner Dispositions, Self-Theories and Student Engagement', *British Journal of Educational Studies 62* (1): 19–35.

DES (Department for Education and Science) (1990) *Starting with Quality (the Rumbold Report of the Committee of Inquiry into the Quality of the Educational Experience Offered to 3- and 4- Year Olds).* London: HMSO.

Desforges, C. (1995) *An Introduction to Teaching: Psychological Perspectives.* Oxford: Blackwell.

De Souza, M. (2004) 'Teaching for Connectedness and Meaning: The Role of Spirituality in the Learning Process', *Panorama, International Journal of Comparative Religious Education and Values 16*: 56–67.

Dewey, J. (1916, 2002) *Democracy and Education.* New York: Free Press.

Dewey, J. (2002) *Human Nature and Conduct.* Mineola: Dover.

Donaldson, M. (1992) *Human Minds – an Exploration.* London: Allen Lane.

Dweck, C. S. (2000) *Self Theories: Their Role in Motivation, Personality and Development.* Philadelphia, PA: Psychology Press.

Eaude, T. (2004) *Values Education: Developing Positive Attitudes.* Birmingham: National Primary Trust.

Eaude, T. (2007*) SMSC- Optional Extras or Hidden Opportunities*? Available at: http://www.nationaleducationtrust.net/ShapingIdeasShapingLives032.php.

Eaude, T. (2008a) *Children's Spiritual, Moral, Social and Cultural Development – Primary and Early Years.* Exeter: Learning Matters.

Eaude, T. (2008b) 'Should Religious Educators be wary of Values Education?' *Journal of Religious Education 56* (3): 57–65.

Eaude, T. (2009) 'Happiness, Emotional Well-Being and Mental Health – What Has Children's Spirituality to Offer?' *International Journal of Children's Spirituality 14* (3): 185–96.

Eaude, T. (2011) *Thinking through Pedagogy for Primary and Early Years.* Exeter: Learning Matters.

Eaude, T. (2012) *How Do Expert Primary Classteachers Really Work? A Critical Guide for Teachers, Headteachers and Teacher Educators.* Northwich: Critical Publishing. Available at: www.criticalpublishing.com.

Eaude, T. (2014) 'Creating Hospitable Space to Nurture Children's Spirituality-Possibilities and Dilemmas Associated with Power', *International Journal of Children's Spirituality 19* (3/4): 236–48.

Ecclestone, K. and D. Hayes (2008) *The Dangerous Rise of Therapeutic Education.* London: Routledge.

Erricker, C. and J. Erricker (2000) *Reconstructing Religious, Spiritual and Moral Education.* London: RoutledgeFalmer.

Erikson, E. (1968) *Identity: Youth and Crisis.* London: Faber and Faber.

Evans, D. (2001) *Emotion – a Very Short Introduction.* Oxford: Oxford University Press.

Farrer, F. (2000) *A Quiet Revolution.* London: Rider.

Fox, R. (2005) *Teaching and Learning: Lessons from Psychology.* Oxford: Blackwell.

Frowe, I. (2007) '"The Politics of Faith and the Politics of Scepticism": Michael Oakeshott, Education and Extremism', *British Journal of Educational Studies 55* (3): 264–85.

Fullan, M. (2003a) *The Moral Imperative of School Leadership.* Thousand Oaks, CA: Corwin.

Fullan, M. (2003b) *Changes Forces with a Vengeance.* London: RoutledgeFalmer.

Geake, J. (2009) *The Brain at School; Educational Neuroscience in the Classroom.* Maidenhead: Open University Press.

Gerhardt, S. (2004) *Why Love Matters: How Affection Shapes a Baby's Brain.* Hove: Brunner Routledge.

Gerhardt, S. (2010) *The Selfish Society: How We All Forgot to Love One Another and Made Money Instead.* London: Simon and Schuster.

Gilligan, C. (1982) *In a Different Voice.* Cambridge, MA: Harvard University Press.

Goldberg, S. (2000) *Attachment and Development.* London: Hodder Arnold.

Goleman, D. (1996) *Emotional Intelligence: Why It Can Matter More Than IQ.* New York: Bloomsbury.

Good, T. L. and J. E. Brophy (1990) *Educational Psychology: A Realistic Approach,* 4th edition. London: Longman.

Goswami, U. and P. Bryant (2010) 'Children's Cognitive Development and Learning', in R. Alexander (ed.), *The Cambridge Primary Review Research Surveys.* Abingdon: Routledge, pp. 141–69.

Graham, L. J. and R. Slee (2008) 'An Illusory Interiority: Interrogating the Discourse/s of Inclusion', *Educational Philosophy and Theory 40* (2): 277–93.

Grayling, A. C. (2001) *The Meaning of Things.* London: Weidenfeld and Nicholson.

Gutmann, A. (1987) *Democratic Education.* Princeton, NJ: Princeton University Press.

Haidt, J. (2012) *The Righteous Mind: Why Good People Are Divided by Politics and Religion.* London: Penguin.

Halstead, J. M. (1996) 'Values and Values Education in Schools', in J. M. Halstead and M. J. Taylor (eds), *Values in Education and Education in Values.* London: Falmer, pp. 3–14.

Hargreaves, A. (2003) *Teaching in the Knowledge Society – Education in the Age of Insecurity.* Maidenhead: Open University Press.

Harris, P. L. (1989) *Children and Emotion.* Oxford: Blackwell.

Hart, S., A. Dixon, M. J. Drummond and D. McIntyre (2004) *Learning without Limits.* Maidenhead: Open University Press.

Harter, S. (1999) *The Construction of the Self: A Developmental Perspective.* New York: Guilford Press.

Hattie, J. (2009) *Visible Learning: A Synthesis of Over 800 Meta-Analyses Relating to Achievement.* London: Routledge.

Haun, D. and M. Tomasello (2011) 'Conformity to Peer Pressure in Preschool Children', *Child Development 82* (6): 1759–67.

Haydon, G. (2004) 'Values Education: Sustaining the Ethical Environment', *Journal of Moral Education 33* (2): 115–29.

Heath, S. B. (2010) 'Play in Nature: The Foundation of Creative Thinking', in C. Tims (ed.), *Born Creative*, pp. 115–25. Available at: www.demos.co.uk/files/Born_Creative_-_web_-_final.pdf.

Hill, B. V. (1981) 'Teacher Commitment and the Ethics of Teaching for Commitment', in G. Rossiter (ed.), *Religious Education in Australian Schools.* Canberra: Curriculum Development Centre, pp. 179–85.

Holloway, R. (2004) *Godless Morality.* Edinburgh: Canongate Books.

Hull, J. (2001) *On Sight and Insight – a Journey into the World of Blindness.* Oxford: One World.

Hyde, B. (2008) *Children and Spirituality: Searching for Meaning and Connectedness.* London: Jessica Kingsley.

Hyde, B. (2009) 'Dangerous Games- Play and Pseudo Play in Religious Education', *Journal of Religious Education 57* (2): 37–46.

Ireson J., P. Mortimore and S. Hallam (1999) 'The Common Strands of Pedagogy and Their Implications', P. Mortimore (ed.), *Understanding Pedagogy and Its Impact on Learning.* London: Paul Chapman, pp. 212–32.

Jackson, P. W., R. E. Boostrom and D. T. Hansen (1993) *The Moral Life of Schools.* San Francisco, CA: Jossey Bass.

Kagan, J. (1994) *Galen's Prophecy.* London: Free Association Books.

Katayama, K. (2004) 'The Virtue Approach to Moral Education', in J. Dunne, and P. Hogan (eds) *Education and Practice – Upholding the Integrity of Teaching and Learning.* Oxford: Blackwell, pp. 61–73.

Katz, L. (2003) 'Current issues and Trends in Early Childhood Education', in T. S. Saraswathi (ed.), *Cross Cultural Perspectives in Human Development: Theory, Research and Application.* London: Sage, pp. 354–82.

Katz, L. G. and J. D. Raths (1985) 'Dispositions as Goals for Teacher Education', *Teaching and Teacher Education 1* (4): 301–7.

Kimes Myers, B. (1997) *Young Children and Spirituality.* London: Routledge.

Kohlberg, L. (1981) *The Philosophy of Moral Development: Moral Stages and the Idea of Justice.* San Francisco, CA: Harper and Row.

Kohlberg, L. (1987) *Child Psychology and Childhood Education: A Cognitive-Developmental View.* New York: Longman.

Kristjansson, K. (2013) 'Ten Myths about Character, Virtue and Virtue Education – Plus Three Well-Founded Misgivings', *British Journal of Educational Studies 61* (3): 269–87.

Lawson, J. and H. Silver (1973) *A Social History of English Education.* London: Methuen.

Layard, R. (2005) *Happiness.* London: Allen Lane.

Layard, R. and J. Dunn (2009) *A Good Childhood – Searching for Values in a Competitive Age.* London: Penguin.

Lickona, T. (1992) *Educating for Character: How Our Schools Can Teach Respect and Responsibility.* New York: Bantam.

Lovat, T. and R. Toomey (ed.) (2007) *Values Education and Quality Teaching: The Double Helix Effect.* Sydney: David Barlow.

Macintyre, A. (1999) *After Virtue.* London: Duckworth.

Maslow, A. (1970) *Motivation and Personality.* New York: Harper and Row.

Mayall, B. (2010) 'Children's Lives Outside School and Their Educational Impact', in R. Alexander (ed.), *The Cambridge Primary Review Research Surveys.* Abingdon: Routledge, pp. 49–82.

McLaughlin, T. H. and J. M. Halstead (1999) 'Education in Character and Virtue', in J. M. Halstead and T. H. McLaughlin (eds), *Education in Morality.* London: Routledge, pp. 132–63.

McMahon, L. (1992) *The Handbook of Play Therapy.* London: Routledge.

Mercer, N. (2000) *Words and Minds – How We Use Words to Think Together.* London: Routledge.

Mill, J. S. (1909) *Autobiography,* Harvard Classics 25, edited by C. E. Norton. New York: P. F. Collier & Son.

National Framework for Values Education in Australian Schools (2005) Available at: http://apo.org.au/research/national-framework-values-education-australian-schools.

Noddings, N. (1991) 'Stories in Dialogue: Caring and Interpersonal Reasoning', in C. Witherell and N. Noddings (eds), *Stories Lives Tell: Narrative and Dialogue in Education.* New York: Teachers' College Press, pp. 157–70.

Noddings, N. (2003) *Happiness and Education.* Cambridge: Cambridge University Press.

Noddings, N. (2005) 'Identifying and Responding to Needs in Education', *Cambridge Journal of Education* 35 (2): 147–59.

Noddings, N. (2013) *Caring – a Relational Approach to Ethics and Moral Education.* Berkeley: University of California Press.

Nouwen, H. J. M. (1996) *Reaching Out: The Three Movements of the Spiritual Life.* London: Fount.

Nussbaum, M. (2001) *The Fragility of Goodness.* New York: Princeton University Press.

Nussbaum, M. (2010) *Not for Profit: Why Democracy Needs the Humanities.* Princeton, NJ: Princeton University Press.

OECD (Organisation for Economic Co-operation and Development) (2007) *Understanding the Brain: The Birth of a Learning Science.* OECD Publishing. Available at: http://dx.doi.org/10.1787/9789264029132-en.

Palmer, P. J. (1983, 1993) *To Know as We Are Known. Education as a Spiritual Journey.* San Francisco, CA: HarperSan Francisco.

Palmer, S. (2006) *Toxic Childhood.* London: Orion Books.

Parker-Rees, R. (2007) 'Liking to Be Liked: Imitation, Familiarity and Pedagogy in the First Years of Life', *Early Years* 27 (1): 3–17.

Patten, K. E. (2011) 'The Somatic Appraisal Model of Affect Paradigm for Educational Neurscience and Neuropedagogy', in K. E. Patten and S. R. Campbell (eds), *Educational Neuroscience – Initiatives and Emerging Issues.* Oxford: Wiley-Blackwell, pp. 86–96.

Piaget, J. (1932) *The Moral Judgment of the Child.* London: Kegan Paul, Trench, Trubner.

Pollard, A. (1985) *The Social World of the Primary School.* London: Cassell.

Pring, R. (2001) 'Education as a Moral Practice', *Journal of Moral Education* 30 (2): 101–12.

Pring, R. (2014) *John Dewey: A Philosopher of Education for Our Own Time?* London: Bloomsbury.

Putnam, R. D. (2000) *Bowling Alone: The Collapse and Revival of American Community.* New York: Simon & Schuster.

Rizzolatti, G. and L. Craighero (2004) 'The Mirror-Neuron System', *Annual Review of Neuroscience 27*: 169–96.

Rogoff, B. (1990) *Apprenticeship in Thinking – Cognitive Development in Social Context.* Oxford: Oxford University Press.

Rowley, S. J., B. Kurtz-Costes, R. Mistry and L. Feagans (2007) 'Social Status as a Predictor of Race and Gender Stereotypes in Late Childhood and Early Adolescence', *Social Development 16* (1): 150–68.

Russell, J. (2007) *How Children Become Moral Selves – Building Character and Promoting Citizenship Education.* Eastbourne: Sussex Academic Press.

Salmon, P. (1995) *Psychology in the Classroom – Reconstructing Teachers and Learners.* London: Cassell.

Salzberger-Wittenberg, I., G. Henry and E. Osborne (1983) *The Emotional Experience of Learning and Teaching.* London: Routledge.

Sawyer, R. K. (2004) 'Creative Teaching: Collaborative Discussion as Disciplined Improvisation', *Educational Researcher 33* (2): 12–20.

Scheindlin, L. (2003) 'Emotional Perception and Spiritual Development', *International Journal of Children's Spirituality 8* (2): 179–93.

Schonert-Reichl, K., V. Smith, A. Zaidman-Zait and C. Hertzman (2012) 'Promoting Children's Prosocial Behaviors in School: Impact of the "Roots of Empathy" Program on the Social and Emotional Competence of School-Aged Children', *School Mental Health 4*: 1–21.

Sennett, R. (1998) *The Corrosion of Character.* New York: W. W. Norton.

Sergiovanni, T. (2001) *Leadership – What's in It for Schools?* London: RoutledgeFalmer.

Shulman, L. S. (2004) *The Wisdom of Practice – Essays on Teaching, Learning and Learning to Teach.* San Francisco, CA: Jossey Bass.

Siraj-Blatchford, I. (1999) 'Early Childhood Pedagogy: Practice, Principles and Research', in P. Mortimore (ed.), *Understanding Pedagogy and Its Impact on Learning.* London: Paul Chapman, pp. 20–45.

Smith, R. and P. Standish (eds) (1997) *Teaching Right and Wrong – Moral Education in the Balance.* Stoke-on-Trent: Trentham Books.

Swing, L. E., D. A. Gentile, C. A. Anderson and D. A. Walsh (2010) 'Television and Video Game Exposure and the Development of Attention Problems', *Pediatrics 126* (2): 214–21.

Symington, N. (1986) *The Analytic Experience.* London: Free Association Books.

Tacey, D. (2004) *The Spirituality Revolution.* Hove: Brunner-Routledge.

Tassoni, P. and K. Hucker (2005) *Planning Play and the Early Years.* Oxford: Heinemann.

Taylor, C. (1989) *Sources of the Self.* Cambridge: Cambridge University Press.

Thompson, R. A. (2009) 'Early Foundations: Conscience and the Development of Moral Character', in D. Narváez and D. K. Lapsley (eds), *Personality, Identity and Character: Explorations in Moral Psychology*. Cambridge: Cambridge University Press, pp. 159–84.

TLRP (Teaching and Learning Research Programme) (2006) *Improving Teaching and Learning in Schools*. London: TLRP. Available at: http://www.tlrp.org/themes/themes/tenprinciples.html.

TLRP (2007) *Neuroscience and Education: Issues and Opportunities*. London: TLRP. Available at: http://www.tlrp.org/pub/commentaries.html.

Trickey, S. and K. J. Topping (2004) '"Philosophy for Children": A Systematic Review', *Research Papers in Education 19* (3): 365–80.

Unicef (2007) *Child Poverty in Perspective: An Overview of Child Well-Being in Rich Countries: A Comparative Assessment of the Lives and Well-Being of Children and Adolescents in Economically Advanced Nations*. Florence, Unicef Innocenti Centre (Innocenti Report Card 7). Available at: http://www.unicef-irc.org/publications/pdf/rc7_Eng.pdf.

United Nations Convention on the Rights of the Child (UNCRC). Available at: www.unicef.org/crc/files/Rights_overview.pdf.

Vygotsky, L. S. (1978) *Mind in Society: The Development of Higher Psychological Processes*. Cambridge, MA: Harvard University Press.

Wall, J. (2010) *Ethics in Light of Childhood*. Washington, DC: Georgetown University Press.

Warnock, M. (1996) 'Moral Values', J. M. Halstead and M. J. Taylor (eds), *Values in Education and Education in Values*. London: Falmer, pp. 45–53.

Wenger, E. (1998) *Communities of Practice – Learning, Meaning and Identity*. New York: Cambridge University Press.

West-Burnham, J. and V. Huws Jones (2007) *Spiritual and Moral Development in Schools*. London: Continuum.

Wilkinson, R. and K. Pickett (2009) *The Spirit Level – Why More Equal Societies Almost Always Do Better*. London: Allen Lane.

Williams, R. (2000) *Lost Icons*. Edinburgh: T and T Clark.

Williams, R. (2012) *Faith in the Public Square*. London: Bloomsbury.

Wilson, J. (2007) *The Performance of Practice*. London: Karnac.

Winnicott, D. (2002) *Playing and Reality*. Hove: Brunner-Routledge.

Winston, J. (1998) *Drama, Narrative and Moral Education*. London: Falmer.

Index